Internet Essentials
Third Edition

David Clark
Boulder Valley School District

que
E&T

An Imprint of Macmillan Computer Publishing USA

Internet Essentials, Third Edition

Copyright© 1997 by Que® Education and Training

Library of Congress Catalog No: 96-67776

ISBN: 1-57576-348-6

00 99 98 97   4 3 2 1

Interpretation of the printing code: the rightmost double-digit number is the year of the book's printing; the rightmost single-digit number, the number of the book's printing. For example, a printing code of 97-1 shows that the first printing of the book occurred in 1997.

Screens reproduced in this book were created using Collage Plus from Inner Media, Inc., Hollis, NH.

Publisher: Robb Linsky

Product Marketing Manager: Susan L. Kindel

Publishing Director: Diane E. Beausoleil

Manager of Publishing Operations: Linda H. Buehler

Managing Editor: Nancy E. Sixsmith

Development Editor: Ginny Noble

Production Editor: S. A. Hobbs

Technical Editor: Geoff McKim, Indiana University

Copy Editor: Asit J. Patel

Editorial Assistant: Beth Montano

Book Designer: Gary Adair

Production Team: Aleata Howard, Laure Robinson, Scott Tullis, Megan Wade

Indexer: Debra Myers

Composed in *Stone Serif* and *MCPdigital* by Que® Education and Training

About the Author

David Clark is an Internet Trainer and technology instructor for the Boulder Valley School District in Boulder, Colorado. He has trained teachers and students at various sites thoroughout the United States. He is also the author of *The Student's Guide to the Internet* published by Que. When not writing and teaching, he can be found gazing at the stars and pulling weeds at clarkd.bvsd.k12.co.us.

Trademark Acknowledgments

Preface

Que Education and Training is the educational publishing imprint of Macmillan Computer Publishing, the world's leading computer book publisher. Macmillan Computer Publishing books have taught more than 20 million people how to be productive with their computers.

This expertise in producing high-quality computer tutorial and reference books is evident in every Que Education and Training title we publish. The same tried-and-true authoring and product-development process that makes Macmillan Computer Publishing books bestsellers is used to ensure that training materials from Que Education and Training contain the most accurate and most up-to-date information. Experienced and respected software trainers write and review every manuscript to provide class-tested pedagogy. Quality-assurance editors check every keystroke and command in Que Education and Training books to ensure that instructions are clear and precise.

Above all, Macmillan Computer Publishing and, in turn, Que Education and Training, have years of experience in meeting the learning demands of adult learners in business, in school, and at home. We offer tiered courseware that

> ➤ provides broad-based, flexible training for novices through expert users.

> ➤ is anchored in the practical and professional needs of adult learners.

> ➤ includes trainer support in fully annotated *Instructor's Manuals*.

The "Essentials" of Hands-On Learning

The *Essentials* series of applications tutorials are appropriate for use in both corporate training and college classroom settings. The *Essentials* workbooks are ideal for short courses. The *Essentials* manuals enable users to become self-sufficient quickly; encourage self-learning after instruction; maximize learning through clear, complete explanations; and serve as future references. Each *Essentials* module is four-color throughout and is sized at $8\frac{1}{2}\times11$ inches for maximum screen-shot visibility.

Project Objectives list what learners will do and learn from the project.

"Why Would I Do This?" shows learners why this material is essential.

Step-by-Step Tutorials simplify the procedures with large screen shots, captions, and annotations.

If you have problems... anticipates common pitfalls and advises learners accordingly.

Inside Stuff provides tips and shortcuts for more effective applications.

Key Terms are highlighted in the text and defined in the margin when they first appear.

Jargon Watch offers a layperson's view of "technobabble" in easily understandable terms.

Checking Your Skills provides true/false, multiple choice, and completion exercises.

Applying Your Skills contains directed, hands-on exercises to check comprehension and reinforce learning.

Instructor's Manual

If you have adopted this text for use in a college classroom, you will receive, upon request, an *Instructor's Manual* at no additional charge. The manual contains suggested curriculum guides for courses of varying lengths, teaching tips, answers to exercises in the "Applying Your Skills" sections, test questions and answers, data files needed to complete each exercise, and solution files. Please contact your local representative or write to us on school letterhead at Macmillan Computer Publishing, 201 W. 103rd Street, Indianapolis, IN 46290-1907, Attn: Que Education and Training.

Table of Contents at a Glance

Table of Contents

Conventions Used in This Book

The *Essentials* series uses the following conventions to make it easier for you to understand the material:

➤ Text that you are to type appears in color and **boldface**.

➤ Underlined letters in menu names, menu commands, and dialog box options appear in a different color. Examples are the File menu, the Open command, and the File name list box.

➤ Important words or phrases appear in *italic* the first time they are discussed.

➤ *Key terms* are defined in the margin as soon as they are introduced.

➤ On-screen text and messages appear in a `special font`.

➤ *If you have problems...* boxes contain troubleshooting tips that anticipate common pitfalls. These are designed to help you solve your own problems so that you can keep up with the rest of the class.

➤ *Jargon Watch* boxes are used to define a group of key terms used in the project.

➤ *Inside Stuff* boxes contain tips and shortcuts to help you use the application more effectively.

Project

1

Getting Started with the Internet

Objectives

In this project you learn how to:

- ➤ Get Connected to the Internet
- ➤ Connect to the Internet through a Direct Connection
- ➤ Log On to the Internet
- ➤ Change Your Password
- ➤ Log Off the Internet
- ➤ Dial into the Internet

Why Would I Do This?

You can't open a newspaper, turn on your television, or pick up a magazine at the newsstand without seeing something about the Internet. In just the past couple of years, we have seen an exponential number of new users coming online. Everybody from the President of the United States to the Rolling Stones to the guy next door can be found on the Internet. What are they doing?

Being connected to the Internet gives you the ability to:

➤ Communicate with anyone in the world who has a link to the Net

➤ Download software and text files using file transfer protocol (FTP)

➤ Conduct research and search a wide range of online databases

➤ Join in international discussion groups about almost any topic under the sun

➤ Publish your accomplishments on the Net and share them with an international audience

The Net has made these capabilities, and more, available to millions of users worldwide. It is time to find out what all the fuss is about.

Lesson 1: Getting Connected to the Internet

You can connect to the Internet in one of two basic ways: dedicated and dial-up connection.

Server
A computer that all the Internet connections go through.

Dedicated connections, which you tend to see only in computer labs or offices, are permanently wired to the *server*, so you don't have to use a modem to make the connection. Dedicated connections make it possible to use graphical point-and-click interfaces to navigate the Internet. With a dedicated connection, your computer becomes part of the Internet. You have a direct link from your computer to the rest of the world. This line is piped into the lab through an *Ethernet* or another networking scheme. These lines have the potential to move data back and forth quickly.

Ethernet
A common networking scheme used to link computers so that they can share data.

Modem
A device that enables a computer to send and receive data over regular phone lines.

Dial-up connections are connections that you make by dialing the server with a *modem* connected to your desktop computer. Dial-up connections can be further broken down into two types: direct and terminal. Dial-up direct accounts usually go by names such as SLIP or PPP. These accounts let you connect to the server just as if you had a dedicated connection; the only differences are that it's slower and you have to use a modem to connect to the server. With a direct dial-up account, you can use graphical software, such as Microsoft Internet Explorer and Netscape Navigator, to make the Internet easier to navigate.

The kind of connectivity to which you have access depends on several factors, including the following:

The hardware you use. Included in this category are your computer and modem (for dial-up connection).

The wiring connecting the machines to the Internet. Are you dialing in from home on a standard phone line (a dial-up connection), or working from a lab at school that has a direct connection (dedicated connection) into the Internet?

The software on your computer. A wide variety of software can be used to access the Internet. The type of computer that you have, its capabilities, and how you are connecting will all determine what software you use.

When you log on to a direct connection, some of the software you might see include the following:

World Wide Web (WWW) browsers, such as Netscape Navigator and Microsoft Explorer, use graphics, video, and sound. They require a great deal of computing power.

E-mail programs such as Eudora and Pine. (You will probably spend more time with these than with any other Internet utilities.)

IRC (Internet Relay Chat) programs, such as mIRC, enable you to access the IRC and talk interactively with old and potential friends around the world. The IRC allows the users to talk in real time with other users around the globe.

News readers, such as Agent or Newswatcher, enable you to keep up with the latest developments of over 20,000 subject categories.

Telnet utilities, such as NCSA Telnet and QVTNet, permit active connections with other computers around the world. When you establish a Telnet session with another computer, you are logged into that computer and issuing it commands over the phone lines.

Telnet
An Internet protocol that enables a user to establish an active connection with a computer at a remote site.

The task that you want to accomplish determines what kind of software program you should run. In this project, Windows 95 Telnet is used as an example.

In this project, you learn how to access your UNIX prompt. The UNIX prompt is where you will give commands to the computer to begin your Internet activity. At the UNIX prompt, your screen will look the same whether you are using a dedicated or dial-up connection. The lessons in this project are for students who use a dedicated connection. A short lesson is included for those who want to use a dial-up connection.

Lesson 2: Connecting to the Internet through a Direct Connection

If you are working in a lab setting, your computer probably has a direct connection to the Internet. The networking software, hardware, and wiring that is already in place keeps the machine permanently on the net, without the need for a modem. In this lesson you learn how to connect into the Internet using telnet software.

To Connect to the Internet through a Direct Connection

❶ Locate the Telnet utility on your hard drive.

You will be using Windows 95 Telnet for the examples in this project, although there are several other programs you can use. Telneting is a way of creating a connection with another computer on the Internet, such as the one that holds your e-mail.

Figure 1.1
Accessing the Telnet utility.

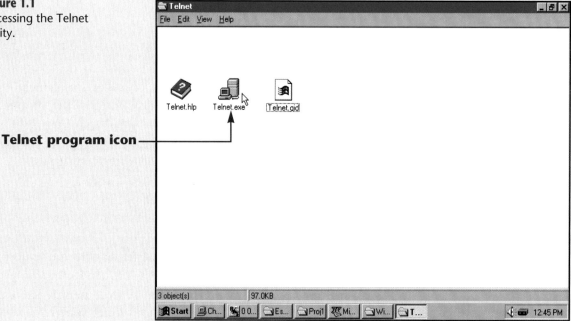

Telnet program icon

❷ Double-click the Telnet program icon.

❸ Choose Remote System from the Connect menu.

It is possible to connect to a number of different computers through Telnet if you know their addresses. For this project, you need to connect with the address in which you have your UNIX account. This address will frequently be the last part of your e-mail address, but not always. Check with your instructor to find the address of the machine where your account resides. An example of an e-mail address is clarkd@bvsd.k12.co.us, so bvsd.k12.co.us would be the address to connect to (see Figure 1.2).

Figure 1.2
Enter the address of the host to which you want to connect.

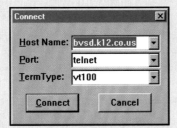

4 Press ⏎Enter.

After the connection is made, you are prompted for your login name and password.

When you apply for an Internet account, you are assigned a *username* (also called a *login name* or *account name*) and a password. Remember them; they are your keys to the Internet. Without a password, you can't access the Internet. Every time you connect to the Internet, you will be prompted for your username and password. The username is permanently assigned to you and becomes part of your e-mail address.

You are now ready to log in. Lesson 3 takes you through that procedure.

It is not necessary to have an Internet account to use software such as Netscape or Agent in a lab with a direct connection. You do need an account, however, to send and receive e-mail.

The following are some other Telnet addresses you can explore:

Telnet	Address
Spacelink (a database of educational activities from NASA)	spacelink.msfc.nasa.gov login: guest
Dartmouth College Library Online Systems	lib.dartmouth.edu
Library of Congress	locis.loc.gov
Weather Underground (weather information for the U.S.)	madlab.sprl.umich.edu 3000
Penpages (for information relating to agriculture, careers, and health and consumer issues)	psupen.psu.edu username: your two-letter state code
Chess servers (for playing interactive chess)	chess.lm.com 5000 Type **g** to enter as a guest

Note that in two of the preceding examples there is a number following the address, such as chess.lm.com 5000. The 5000 is the port number, which refers to the port on the UNIX machine you are connecting with. It is crucial that you include the port number as part of the address to make the connection happen.

Lesson 3: Logging On to the Internet

Whether your connection to the Internet is a dial-up account or through a Telnet utility over a direct connection, you will eventually come to a prompt to fill in your login name and password. Your login name is the first part of your e-mail address. For example, my address is clarkd@bvsd.k12.co.us, and my login name is clarkd.

To Log On to the Internet

❶ Enter your login name when prompted and press ⏎Enter.

You are then prompted for a password. This should have been supplied to you when you applied for an Internet account.

❷ Enter your password and then press ⏎Enter.

For security purposes, passwords do not appear on-screen as you type them.

There may be other steps to your login procedure; each site is slightly different. Make sure you know what the login sequence is for your system. You can ask your instructor or system administrator for this information.

If you have logged on correctly, you will see the UNIX prompt. This is where you can type the commands to read mail, access the World Wide Web, read Netnews, access software archives, and so on.

If you receive a message such as

```
login incorrect
```

you probably mistyped your password or login name. Login names and passwords are case-sensitive and must be typed correctly. Try entering the information again. If it still doesn't work, you may need to ask for assistance. Next, you are ready to change your password.

Lesson 4: Changing Your Password

Changing your password is the first thing you should do when going into your account for the first time. Passwords are private and should never be given out to anyone.

Why all the secrecy? Consider what someone could do with access to your account. In 1994 a hacker broke into a professor's account at Texas A&M

University and distributed 25,000 blatantly racist messages to the rest of the world. That particular faculty member was left holding the bag, and his mailbox was flooded with angry replies. Take steps to protect your password.

To Change Your Password

❶ At the UNIX prompt, type passwd and press ⏎Enter.

You are prompted for your current password (see Figure 1.3).

Figure 1.3
Changing your password.

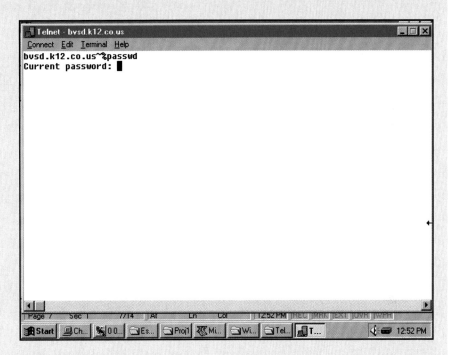

❷ Enter your current password and press ⏎Enter.

UNIX then prompts you for a new password. Passwords are case-sensitive, are usually 6–8 characters, and can include special characters such as $, %, and *. Don't use your name, your birthday, or your pet's name. Examples of good passwords include Blourb6, scor,pio, and $tuition.

❸ Type a new password and press ⏎Enter.

You are then prompted to type the password again for confirmation.

❹ Retype the password and press ⏎Enter.

Your password is now changed. Use this password the next time you log in.

Lesson 5: Logging Off the Internet

When you are finished with your work online, it is time to log off. There is a correct way to end a session.

To Log Off the Internet

❶ At the UNIX prompt, type logout.

Your connection to the Internet is terminated.

❷ Choose Exit from the File menu in Telnet to exit the communications program.

If you have completed your session, check with your instructor for further instructions; otherwise, continue with Lesson 6 or with "Checking Your Skills" at the end of the project.

You can also type **exit** or press Ctrl+D to log off the system.

Lesson 6: Dialing into the Internet

If you have access to a dedicated Internet connection through your college or place of employment, all the software and hardware is in place, and connecting to the Internet is easy. Everything you need is already in place.

However, there are times when you are going to want to dial into the Internet. Generally, you do this from a home computer using a dial-up terminal account (also referred to as a shell account).

Dial-up terminal accounts are pretty basic. When you dial into the server with a terminal account, your computer isn't directly "on" the Internet; it's merely acting as a terminal for the server. You issue your requests to the server, which issues them on your behalf on the Internet.

To do this, you'll need a *communications program*. This program tells your modem what to do when it's communicating with the service provider's computer, and displays to your screen the text you receive and send while working on the Internet.

Service Provider
A company or organization that provides you with Internet access.

A wide variety of communications software is available. Chances are that you already have a communications program on your hard drive to make the necessary connection. If not, a number of good shareware programs can be obtained for modest shareware fees. If you are a Windows user, the terminal program that comes with Windows 3.1 or Windows 95 does an adequate job of getting you hooked up to the Net. Many computers come preloaded with an integrated software package, such as ClarisWorks or Microsoft Works, which includes a communications component.

Even though the computer and modem are similar for terminal and direct accounts, the software you need is different, and the procedures for setting up and using the software are different, too.

To set up a terminal account, all you need to do is select a communications program (almost any program will do), configure it (baud speed, terminal type=vt100, and so on), turn on your modem, and dial.

What to Expect with a Dial-Up Connection

When you dial into a UNIX machine with a terminal account, your computer screen will think, look, and act like that UNIX machine. Everything will be text-based, and your mouse will not work for moving or selecting text in the middle of a paragraph; you will have to use the arrow keys to move around. However, the mouse *will* work with most of the menu items in your communications program, so you can do some basics, such as cut and paste.

To Connect to the Internet through a Dial-Up Connection

❶ Turn on your modem and start your communications software.

❷ Type atdt <your dial-in number>.

The number should have been provided to you when you applied for your Internet account. When you type **at**, you get the modem's attention; **dt** means to dial in the tone mode. If you are using a rotary phone, substitute **dp** (dial pulse). Your modem or software may require other initialization codes. Check with your instructor if you need these.

❸ Press ⏎Enter.

You should now hear your modem dialing, and then the connection being made. A connect message should appear next, as shown in Figure 1.4.

Figure 1.4
Dialing into the Internet.

Connect message ──────

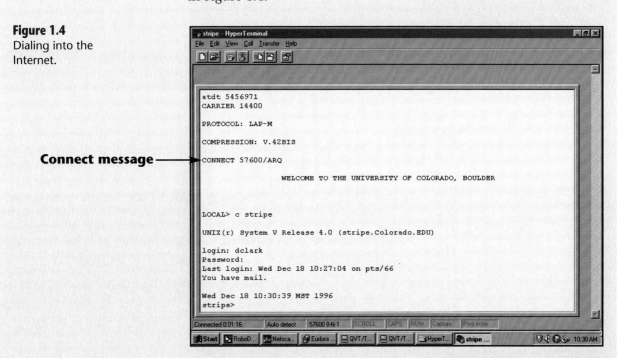

continues

To Connect to the Internet through a Dial-Up Connection (continued)

If you have completed your session, check with your instructor for further instructions; otherwise, continue with "Checking Your Skills" at the end of the project.

SLIP/PPP

With the right hardware and software set up, you are not stuck in the world of text-based information through a dial-up connection. There are two other options to bring video, graphics, and sounds via the Internet over a dial-up connection. You are still limited by the speed of your modem and line, however. That means this type of connection will be slower than with a dedicated link. You can take advantage of all the nifty graphical interfaces and remain within your operating system of choice.

SLIP stands for Serial Line Internet Protocol. PPP stands for Point-to-Point Protocol. These are two different ways of achieving the same thing—to fool the host computer into thinking you have a direct connection. To run a SLIP/PPP account, you will need everything mentioned in the dial-up segment of this chapter, plus the following:

➤ A SLIP or PPP account on your host computer

➤ TCP/IP software installed on your hard drive

Find out first whether your service provider supports SLIP or PPP. If the answer is yes, ask for a SLIP/PPP account. You will also need some additional software and some documentation. The provider should be able to provide you with this as well.

Checking Your Skills

True/False

For each of the following, check *T* or *F* to indicate whether the statement is true or false.

__T __F **1.** Telnet is a way of creating a connection with a remote computer.

__T __F **2.** A modem is required for connecting into the Internet via a direct connection.

__T __F **3.** UNIX is an operating system used by many machines on the Internet.

__T __F **4.** You must have an account on a computer with a direct connection into the Internet in order to be able to receive e-mail.

__T __F **5.** Communications software comes preconfigured and ready to use.

Multiple Choice

Circle the letter of the correct answer for each of the following.

1. Which of the following is a good example of a password?

    a. yellow

    b. 2bontb

    c. telnet

    d. all of the above

2. Which of the following information should you receive when you apply for an Internet account?

    a. a user login

    b. a user password

    c. a dial-in number and login sequence

    d. all of the above

3. It is possible to use graphical interfaces over a dial-up connection by using which of the following?

    a. SLIP

    b. Telnet

    c. PPP

    d. a and c

4. Which of the following is *not* necessary to establish a dial-up connection?

    a. a modem

    b. communications software

    c. an account on a computer directly connected to the Internet

    d. all are necessary

5. Which part of the address clarkd@bvsd.k12.co.us represents the login name?

    a. clarkd

    b. bvsd.k12.co.us

    c. bvsd

    d. co.us

Completion

In the blank provided, write the correct answer for each of the following statements.

1. When telnetting to a remote computer, you are usually prompted for a(n) _____ and a(n) _____.

2. When dialing in to the Internet, the terminal emulation should be set to _____.

3. _____ will not show up on-screen when you type them.

4. bvsd.k12.co.us% is an example of a(n) _____.

5. The most likely reason for receiving the `login incorrect` message when trying to make a connection is _____.

Applying Your Skills

At the end of each project in this book, you can use the "On Your Own" and "Brief Cases" exercises to practice your new Internet skills. Take a few minutes to work through these exercises now.

On Your Own

Searching a Library Database via Telnet

It is possible to create Telnet sessions with other machines, many of which give public access. Libraries frequently let users browse their card catalogs through a Telnet connection.

In this exercise, you connect to the Carl System. Carl offers access to a variety of commercial databases and over 420 public library catalogs.

To Search a Library Database via Telnet

1. At the UNIX prompt, type `telnet pac.carl.org`.

This is the address to which you want to connect. If you are using Wintel, NCSA Telnet, or another Telnet utility, type `pac.carl.org`.

2. Press `↵Enter`.

If the site you are connecting to is a public Telnet site, you will see instructions telling you what to do. If a login name is requested, type `newuser`, `guest`, or `anonymous`. If these don't work, the site is not set up for public access. In this case, you have two choices (see Figure 1.5):

```
EXIT    PAC
```

Figure 1.5
Connecting to a library.

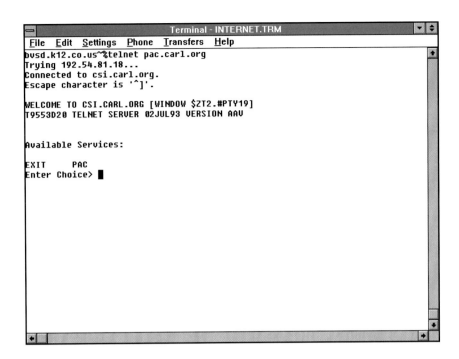

```
┌─────────────────── Terminal - INTERNET.TRM ───────────────── ▼ ◆ ┐
│ File  Edit  Settings  Phone  Transfers  Help                   ↑ │
│ bvsd.k12.co.us~%telnet pac.carl.org                            │
│ Trying 192.54.81.18...                                        │
│ Connected to csi.carl.org.                                    │
│ Escape character is '^]'.                                     │
│                                                               │
│ WELCOME TO CSI.CARL.ORG [WINDOW $ZT2.#PTY19]                  │
│ T9553D20 TELNET SERVER 02JUL93 VERSION AAV                    │
│                                                               │
│                                                               │
│ Available Services:                                          │
│                                                               │
│ EXIT    PAC                                                   │
│ Enter Choice> ▋                                              │
│                                                              ↓ │
└──┐                                                           ┌──┘
   ◆ └                                                       ┘ ◆
```

Typing exit at this point takes you back to the UNIX prompt.

3. Type PAC and press ⏎Enter.

You are then asked to choose from a menu of terminal types .

4. Select 5. VT100 and press ⏎Enter.

From here, you can enter a variety of different library catalogs.

Brief Cases

Navigating an Online Menu System

"Brief Cases" help you learn how the Internet can be used in a business situation. As you work through this continuing case study, you learn how the Internet can help you run your own business.

If you have already used other books in the Que Education and Training *Essentials* series, you have probably learned how other software applications can help a small, start-up business such as Sound Byte Music, the example used in the "Brief Cases" case study. If you haven't used other *Essentials* books before, imagine that you are the owner and hands-on business manager of Sound Byte Music, a new music store located in a college town.

Information on music abounds on the Internet. As owner of a small business, you need information relating to the financial climate of the market. The Economic Bulletin Board of the United States Department of Commerce is available via Telnet. Logging in and exploring it is a good way to get up-to-date financial information and to learn how to navigate online menu systems.

To Navigate an Online Menu System

1. At the UNIX prompt, type **telnet ebb.stat-usa.gov** and press ⏎Enter.

This is the address to which you want to connect. If you are using a Telnet utility, type **ebb.stat-usa.gov** as the site you want to connect to; then press ⏎Enter.

2. Log in as **guest** (see Figure 1.6) and follow the on-screen instructions.

Figure 1.6
The Economic Bulletin Board.

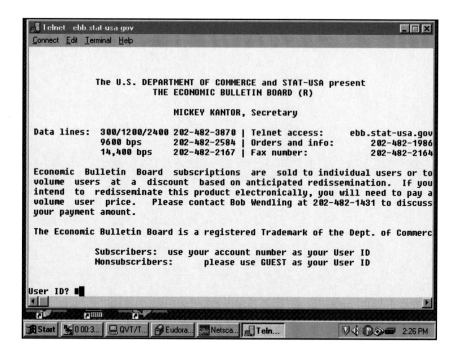

3. Press ⏎Enter.

4. Spend some time exploring the resources on this bulletin board.

Project 2

Using E-Mail

Objectives

In this project you learn how to:

➤ Start Pine
➤ Navigate Pine's Menu-Driven Mailing System
➤ Send an E-Mail Message
➤ Read the Mail in Your Mailbox
➤ Reply, Forward, Save, and Delete Mail
➤ Print an E-Mail Message
➤ Create a Signature File
➤ Create an Address Book

Why Would I Do This?

The ability to communicate with anyone who has an e-mail address and to do it with the immediacy that e-mail provides is nothing short of a revolution. It has changed the way we do business and the way we study and go to school.

The sophistication and speed of our personal communications has steadily increased over the years. Less than 100 years ago, a letter may have taken weeks before being delivered; push that back a few more years, and the time scale moves from weeks to months. From the invention of the telegraph right on through to the formation of Federal Express, we have looked for ways to move our thoughts across space with more speed and efficiency.

An e-mail message can travel from North America to Antarctica in less than a second, and not much longer than that to travel all around the world with optimum conditions and connections. When set up properly, e-mail is more immediate and more precise than other forms of communication.

Many different programs are used to send and receive e-mail. In this project, you learn how to send and receive e-mail by using the Pine mailing program. Most of the other programs that can be used to send e-mail have the same features as Pine. Some of the more popular mailing programs you might encounter include UNIX Mail, Elm, and Eudora.

Lesson 1: Starting Pine

In order to send and receive e-mail on the Internet, you need to have an account on a computer directly tied into the Internet. UNIX is the most common operating system used today on the Internet. Pine is a UNIX-based mailing program that has become popular with users on the Internet. UNIX is easy to use and has a menu-driven system that makes it easy to navigate. You start Pine from the UNIX prompt. Pine will work with a dial-up connection or a Telnet utility over a direct connection, as described in Project 1. If you don't know how to get to the UNIX prompt, see the Appendix, "UNIX—What You Need to Know" at the end of this book.

This book discusses Pine 3.95, the most current version of Pine at the time this book was published. If your system is using an older version, you may notice slight variations in what you see on your screen.

To Start Pine

① Access the UNIX prompt.

If you are in a lab setting with a direct connection to the Internet, this means that you are using a Telnet program to connect with your server. If you are working with a dial-up connection, use your communications software and modem to dial into your server.

❷ At the UNIX prompt, type pine.

The UNIX prompt is different on every system. For this project, the prompt is one found at the University of Colorado, as shown in Figure 2.1.

Figure 2.1
Typing **pine** at the UNIX prompt loads the program.

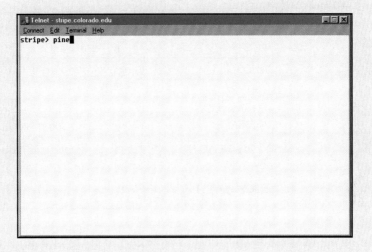

❸ Press ⏎Enter.

After you press ⏎Enter, the computer loads the program and displays the Pine main menu, as shown in Figure 2.2.

From the Pine main menu, you can make choices according to what you want to do. Because Pine works in a terminal emulation mode, the commands you issue are actually being issued to the computer you are connected to. Usually, this means that you are stuck with using only your keyboard to tell the computer what you want to do. Forget the mouse; it won't work. To make your selection, you can either use the arrow keys to move to the option you want to activate, or type the letter shown in the left column.

Figure 2.2
The main menu you see when you first start Pine.

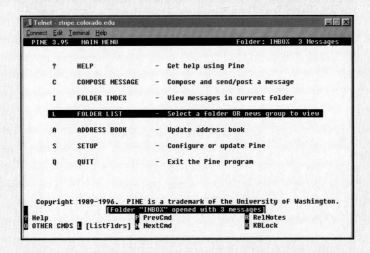

Lesson 2: Navigating Pine's Menu-Driven Mailing System

Pine offers you seven choices from its main menu. Table 2.1 describes each of the choices.

Table 2.1	Parts of the Pine Main Menu
Menu Choice	Description
? HELP	Brings up a help menu where additional online help can be found.
C COMPOSE MESSAGE	Brings up a window in which you can enter pertinent information to compose and send a new e-mail message.
I FOLDER INDEX	Takes you to your mail index, where all your incoming e-mail is stored.
L FOLDER LIST	Takes you to your folders. Pine allows users to save mail in different folders.
A ADDRESS BOOK	Creates an address book. In your address book, you can put the addresses of the people you frequently correspond with.
S SETUP	Used to personalize your Pine settings. Pine offers many different options that you can set by bringing up this window.
Q QUIT	Exits Pine and returns you to the UNIX prompt.

To access any of the items on the main menu, you simply type the letter or use your arrow keys to select the item, and then press ⏎Enter. Notice the top menu item, ? HELP, which provides online help in Pine. In this lesson, you access the Pine help menu.

To Access the Pine Help Menu

❶ From the Pine main menu, press ⑦.

The Pine help menu is displayed, as shown in Figure 2.3. You can access the help menu at any point while you are in Pine, except while composing a message.

❷ Explore the Pine help options by using the Spacebar to move to the next page of text.

Additional commands are listed at the bottom of the Pine main menu. When you are in your inbox or composing or reading mail, the menu at the bottom of the window will help you if you can't remember the correct commands.

Figure 2.3
The Pine help menu.

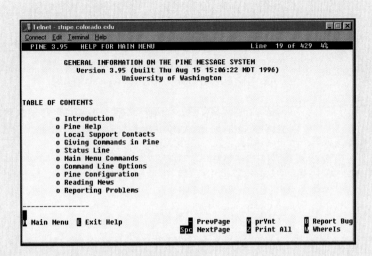

❸ When you are finished, press Ⓔ.

This exits the help menu and returns you to the Pine main menu.

Lesson 3: Sending an E-Mail Message

In this lesson, you take a look at what constitutes an e-mail address. Understanding the syntax of an address can be helpful and prevents you from making mistakes. Addresses must be exact; they cannot include spaces or spelling errors. In this lesson, you compose and send a message to the President of the United States.

Anatomy of an E-Mail Address

Sending e-mail is a simple task as long as you know the address of the person you want to send it to. E-mail addresses make sense if you know how to take them apart. An e-mail address is a combination of letters, numbers, and symbols. They almost always include an @ sign and some periods. Table 2.2 breaks down my e-mail address with the Boulder Valley School District:

```
clarkd@bvsd.k12.co.us
```

Table 2.2 Examination of an E-Mail Address	
clarkd	The login name used when I connect to the Internet.
@	Every internet e-mail address has one of these in it.
bvsd	The name of the computer I am connected to.
k12	The school district I work for services kindergarten through 12th grade.
co	That school district is in Colorado. . .
us	. . . and in the United States.

The information before the @ sign is the username; the information after @ gives the location. Not all e-mail addresses are easy to read.

You can tell a lot from an e-mail address. For example, sometimes you can tell which country someone is from by the suffix in the address. Table 2.3 lists just a few geographical e-mail suffixes.

Table 2.3	Geographical Explanation of E-Mail Suffixes
Suffix	Location
au	Australia
at	Austria
ca	Canada
de	Germany
dk	Denmark
fi	Finland
fr	France
uk	United Kingdom
us	United States

Not all addresses are geographically designed. Some e-mail addresses tell you the nature of the organization. For example, the address

```
dclark@mcp.com
```

is a valid e-mail address. The .com at the end tells you that mcp is a commercial site on the Internet. (In this case, it's the site of my publisher's parent company, Macmillan Computer Publishing.) If your connection is through your school or university, there is a good chance that your e-mail address ends in .edu, which stands for education. For example, the e-mail address

```
dclark@stripe.colorado.edu
```

tells you that the address is housed at an educational institution.

Table 2.4 lists some other common e-mail suffixes by usage.

Table 2.4	E-Mail Suffixes by Usage
Suffix	Use
gov	Government
com	Commercial organization
mil	Military
net	Network resources
org	Nonprofit organizations (usually)
edu	Educational institution

To Send an E-Mail Message

1 **Load Pine, if it isn't already loaded.**

2 **From the Pine main menu, press Ⓒ.**

A window appears in which you can begin to compose your message (see Figure 2.4).

Figure 2.4
You are ready to compose a message.

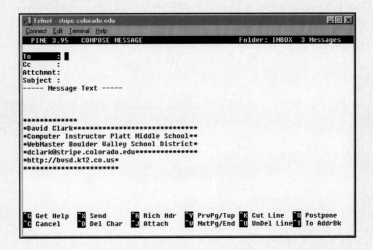

3 **On the To: line, type president@whitehouse.gov and press ⏎Enter.**

This is the President's address, where you are sending the e-mail. If you want to send a copy of the same message to another person, you type that person's e-mail address in the Cc: line.

4 **Leave the Attchmnt: line blank.**

You enter information here when you want to attach another file to your e-mail. You can use this option to send binary files, such as graphics and programs.

5 **In the Subject: line, enter a subject.**

The Subject: line is important. You want your message to stand out. The President receives a great deal of e-mail, and if you want your message to be read, you need a Subject: line that will grab his attention. Mail without a subject heading frequently gets deleted without ever being read.

6 **Press ⏎Enter twice.**

This moves you to the Message Text line, where you compose your message.

7 **Enter your message below the Message Text line and press Ctrl+Ⓧ.**

If you can't think of anything you want to say to the President, you can copy the message in Figure 2.5. The Secret Service takes crank

continues

messages to the White House very seriously, so consider carefully your words if you choose to create your own.

The command Ctrl+X is in the menu at the bottom of the Pine window, except that the command appears as ^X SEND. The ^ sign is the symbol for Ctrl. Whenever you see that symbol preceding a command, you are to press and hold down Ctrl while pressing the character key.

After you press Ctrl+X, Pine asks whether you really want to send the message (see Figure 2.5).

Figure 2.5
You press Y or ↵Enter to send the e-mail message.

8 **Press** Y**.**

Alternatively, you can simply press ↵Enter to send the message. Your first e-mail message is now on its way to Washington, D.C.

If you did everything correctly, you may get a response from the White House in minutes or hours, depending on the mail load on any given day.

Now try sending an e-mail to yourself.

9 **Enter your own e-mail address in the To: line, enter a message, and press** Ctrl+X **to send it.**

Within seconds, the message will appear in your mailbox, and you can use it for Lesson 4, where you learn to read mail in your mailbox.

Pine has a built-in spell checker. Press Ctrl+T to use it.

Lesson 4: Reading the Mail in Your Mailbox

After you have sent an e-mail, you can return to the main menu by pressing Ⓜ. From the main menu, you can go to the folder index where your new mail is stored. When e-mail comes into your inbox folder, you see a listing of the messages. The following is an example of a message:

```
+   4  Mar 15 Corrina Perrone  (1,738) Re: meeting tomorrow - confir-
mation..
```

The + at the beginning of the address lets you know that you are the primary recipient of the e-mail message. There are many mailing lists on the Internet that distribute copies of messages to hundreds and even thousands of people. The + tells you that this is not one of them.

Mar 15 means that the message was sent on March 15th.

Corrina Perrone is the author of the message.

1,738 refers to the length of the message. In this case, the message takes up 1.7K of disk space.

RE: meeting... is the subject heading. When your mailbox becomes full and time is short, look here to decide which messages to read.

Another symbol you frequently see is an N before the number. An N indicates that the message is new and you haven't read it yet.

To Read the Mail in Your Mailbox

❶ Press Ⓘ.

You will have potentially three messages in your mailbox (also referred to as your inbox): a copy of the message you sent to the President (you will have this only if you included your address in the Cc: line), a reply from the White House, and the message you sent to yourself in the preceding lesson. Figure 2.6 shows how your screen should look.

continues

To Read the Mail in Your Mailbox (continued)

Figure 2.6
You should have three messages in your mailbox.

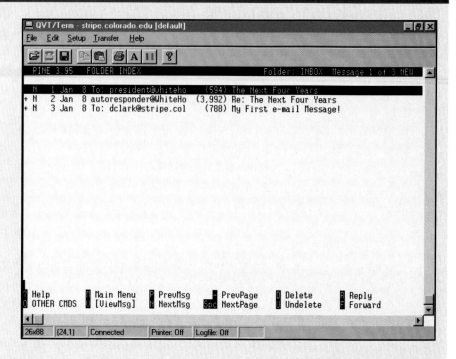

❷ Select a message to read.

To select a message, use the arrow keys or type the number of the message; then press ⏎Enter. If the reply from the President is there, open that message. If not, open one of the others. Figure 2.7 shows an example of a reply from the White House.

Figure 2.7
E-mail from the President.

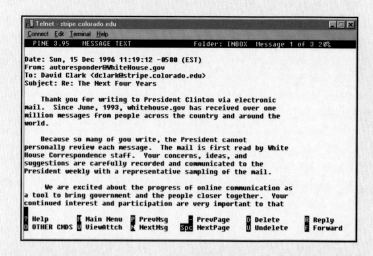

❸ Press Spacebar **to view the rest of the message.**

The spacebar will move you to the next page of text. If you want to go up a page, press ⊟.

❹ When you've finished reading the message, press Ⅰ.

This takes you back to your folder index where you can select another message to read.

The other commands found on the main menu will work here as well. For example, from within this message from the President, you can press ⓠ to quit Pine or ⓜ to return to the main menu.

Lesson 5: Replying, Forwarding, Saving, and Deleting Mail

After you have read your e-mail, it is time to decide what to do with it. You have four options: reply to the message, forward the message to another person on the Internet, save the mail to a folder, or delete the mail.

To Reply to a Message

❶ **Open a message in your mailbox. With the message displayed on-screen, press Ⓡ.**

Pine asks whether you want to include the original message in your reply.

❷ **Press Ⓨ.**

This indicates that you want to include a copy of the message in your reply. Including a copy is a good idea if you are referring to something in the original message. You press Ⓝ to reply without including a copy of the original message.

Pine then fills in the address and adds the Subject: line for you. If you want to change the subject, use the arrow keys to move to the subject, delete it, and then enter your own.

❸ **Type your message and press Ⓒⓣⓡⓛ+Ⓧ.**

Pressing Ctrl+X sends your message. Pine returns you to your original message, and you are ready for the next lesson.

When you want to send a copy of the message to another user, use the forwarding function.

To Forward a Message

❶ **Open a message in your mailbox. With the message displayed on-screen, press Ⓕ.**

Pine loads the message into the Forward Message window.

❷ **In the To: line, enter the e-mail address where you want the message sent.**

Again, Pine fills in the subject followed by (fwd), indicating that it is a forwarded message. If you want, you can add comments to the message before you send it.

continues

To Forward a Message (continued)

❸ **Press** Ctrl+X.

This step sends your message. When Pine displays the prompt to send the message, press Y. Figure 2.8 shows an example of a forwarded message.

Figure 2.8
A forwarded message
ready to be sent.

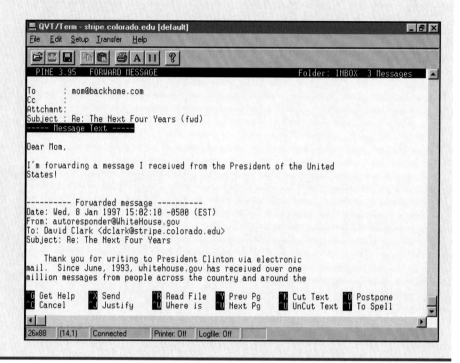

```
QVT/Term - stripe.colorado.edu [default]                        _ |8|×|
File   Edit   Setup   Transfer   Help

  PINE 3.95    FORWARD MESSAGE                  Folder: INBOX   3 Messages

To      : mom@backhome.com
Cc      :
Attchmnt:
Subject : Re: The Next Four Years (fwd)
----- Message Text -----

Dear Mom,

I'm forwarding a message I received from the President of the United
States!


---------- Forwarded message ----------
Date: Wed, 8 Jan 1997 15:02:10 -0500 (EST)
From: autoresponder@WhiteHouse.gov
To: David Clark <dclark@stripe.colorado.edu>
Subject: Re: The Next Four Years

     Thank you for writing to President Clinton via electronic
mail.  Since June, 1993, whitehouse.gov has received over one
million messages from people across the country and around the

^G Get Help   ^X Send       ^R Read File   ^Y Prev Pg   ^K Cut Text   ^O Postpone
^C Cancel     ^J Justify     ^W Where is    ^V Next Pg   ^U UnCut Text ^T To Spell

26x88    (14,1)    Connected         Printer: Off   Logfile: Off
```

At times, you will want to save a copy of a received message but don't want to have to look at it every time you enter your mailbox. Organizing your mail into folders will keep your mailbox cleaned out and aid you in locating saved mail.

To Save Your Mail to a Folder

❶ **Select a message to save to a folder.**

❷ **With the message displayed on your screen, press** S.

Pine prompts you to fill in a folder name.

❸ **Type the name of the folder in which you want to store the message.**

If the folder doesn't exist, Pine asks whether you want to create it:

Folder "new.folder" in <mail/[]> doesn't exist. Create?

❹ **Press** Y.

The mail is transferred into that folder. The folders can then be accessed from the main menu.

5 **Press** Ⓜ.

This returns you to the main menu.

6 **Select FOLDER LIST and then press** ⏎Enter.

The Folder List window appears. Figure 2.9 shows an example of the Folder List window.

Figure 2.9
The Folder List window.

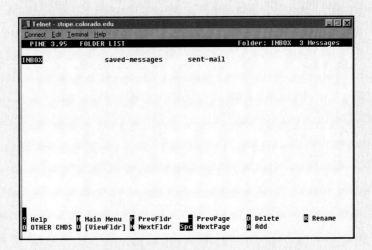

7 **Use the arrow keys to select the folder you want to open; then press** ⏎Enter.

The folder is opened, and your saved mail appears. From here, you can read your mail and then return to the main menu by pressing Ⓜ, just as in any other Pine session.

You can access your folders at any time by pressing Ⓖ. Pine then prompts you for the name of the folder you want to open. Type the name of the folder and press ⏎Enter.

Sometimes you are going to want to delete your mail. Each message takes up space on the hard drive of your host computer. If there is no reason to keep the message, delete it.

To Delete Mail

1 **From your inbox, select a message that you want to delete.**

You can select a message for deletion while you are viewing the messages in your inbox or in a saved message folder. You can delete a message while viewing it on-screen or in your message inbox.

2 **Press** Ⓓ.

If you delete a message on-screen, Pine will display the next message on your screen. If you delete a message while in your inbox, a D appears in front of the message.

continues

To Delete Mail (continued)

When you press Ⓓ, the message is not deleted immediately. When you exit Pine, the following prompt appears:

```
Expunge 1 message from INBOX?
```

❹ Press Ⓨ.

This deletes the message.

If you want a hard copy of your e-mail message, you can get a copy using Pine as well. The next lesson shows you how.

It is possible to delete mail without quitting Pine. If you have marked mail for deletion, Press Ⓧ. Pine will ask you the following:

```
Expunge the 1 deleted message from INBOX?
```

Press Ⓨ, and the mail will be deleted. Press Ⓝ to leave the message in your inbox.

You can undelete the message from your inbox by pressing Ⓤ while the message is highlighted.

Lesson 6: Printing an E-Mail Message

Pine enables you to send e-mail directly to your desktop printer. First, it may be necessary to configure Pine to be able to use this function.

If you have problems...

Printing directly from Pine doesn't work on every system. If you are working from a dial-up connection, not all communications software supports this feature. If your message isn't sent to your printer, try finding different software to dial in with.

To Print Your E-Mail

❶ Press Ⓜ.

This returns you to the main menu. Next, you need to display the Setup window so that you can configure Pine to print.

❷ Press Ⓢ.

The Setup window is displayed. Pine prompts you to choose a task.

❸ Press Ⓟ.

This step brings up a window where you can set your printing options (see Figure 2.10).

Figure 2.10
Configuring Pine to
print your message.

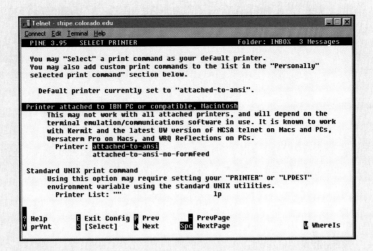

The attached-to-ansi option will be selected for you.

4 Press ⏎Enter.

This step tells Pine that you want to print using the printer attached to your desktop computer.

5 Press E **to exit the Pine Setup window.**

6 Press I.

This returns you to the inbox. Now you are ready to select a message to print.

7 Select a message to print.

8 Press Y.

This command instructs Pine to print your message. The following prompt appears:

```
Print message 4 using "attached-to-ansi"?
```

9 Press Y.

The selected e-mail message is printed.

If you have problems...

If your e-mail message doesn't print, select the entire message on your screen. In your communications software menu, look under the File menu. Many software packages have a "print selection" command. Use this command to send your mail to the printer.

---

10 Press M **to return to the main menu.**

In the next lesson, you learn how to create a signature file.

Lesson 7: Creating a Signature File

A *signature file* is a personalized message that is attached to the end of every e-mail message you send. A signature file should be no longer than four to six lines and may contain your name, title (optional), e-mail address, a favorite quote (optional), and a design created using symbols on your keyboard (optional).

To create and design a signature file, you must first open a new document using a UNIX text editor from the UNIX prompt. A popular text editor on most UNIX systems is called *pico*. Pico is the same editor that Pine uses when you compose an e-mail message.

Signature files are commonly referred to as .signature, pronounced *dot-signature*.

To Create a Signature File

❶ **From the Pine main menu, press Ⓢ to display the Setup window.**

❷ **Press Ⓢ again.**

This starts the text editor pico and displays a blank page, where you can create your signature file.

❸ **Create your signature file.**

Use any of the keys and symbols on your keyboard to design your signature file. Try to be creative. Figure 2.11 shows an example of a signature file.

Figure 2.11
A signature file created in pico.

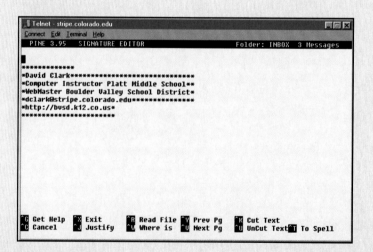

❹ **Press Ctrl+Ⓧ.**

This exits you from pico, and you are returned to the Pine main menu. The next time you send e-mail, Pine will attach your signature file to the end of your e-mail message.

Lesson 8: Creating an Address Book

If you have people who you frequently exchange e-mail with, you can put them in your e-mail address book. The advantage to doing this is that you won't have to remember their e-mail addresses every time you want to write them. Pine will fill in the address for you.

To Add an Entry to Your Address Book

1 From the Pine main menu, press Ⓐ.

You go into your address book.

2 Press Ⓐ again.

This time the a command instructs Pine that you want to make a new addition to your address book. You will see a screen such as in Figure 2.12

Figure 2.12
Creating an entry in your address book.

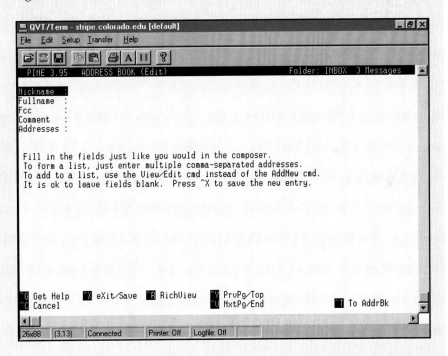

3 Beside Nickname: type President and press ↵Enter.

The nickname will be the name you want to type instead of the full e-mail address.

4 Beside Fullname: type Bill Clinton and press ↵Enter.

You can ignore the Fcc: and Comment: lines and skip down to the Addresses: line.

5 Beside Address: type president@whitehouse.gov and press Ctrl+Ⓧ. Pine will then ask you:

Exit and Save Changes?

continues

To Add an Entry to Your Address Book (continued)

6 Type Ⓨ.

The President of the United States is now in your address book. The next time you want to send him e-mail, simply fill in **President** in the To: line in Pine. Pine will look up the address and fill it in for you.

7 Press Ⓜ to return to the Pine main menu.

You can simplify this procedure by pressing Ⓣ while you have a message on-screen from someone you want to add to your address book. Pine will automatically add the address to your address book and prompt you for a nickname.

It is also possible in Pine to assign a single nickname to a group of people. Then, when you type the nickname in the To: line in Pine, your e-mail will go out to a group of people. In the next exercise, you make an entry for other people in your class. (If you are not taking a class, choose four or five acquaintances to use.)

To Assign a Nickname to a Group

1 From the Pine main menu, press Ⓐ to access your address book.

2 Press Ⓐ again create a new entry.

Pine provides the following prompt:

```
Longname/description of new list:
```

3 Beside Nickname: type class and press ↵Enter.

This is the nickname you will use to send a mailing to everyone in your class. Skip the Fullname: and Fcc: fields and move down to the Comment: line.

4 Beside Comment: type Internet Class and press ↵Enter.

This is a reference for yourself to help you remember what this list means.

5 Beside Addresses: fill in the first e-mail address followed by a comma.

Repeat this procedure as many times as it takes to include everybody in the list that you want included remembering to put a comma between each e-mail address as shown in Figure 2.13.

Figure 2.13
Creating a mailing list in Pine.

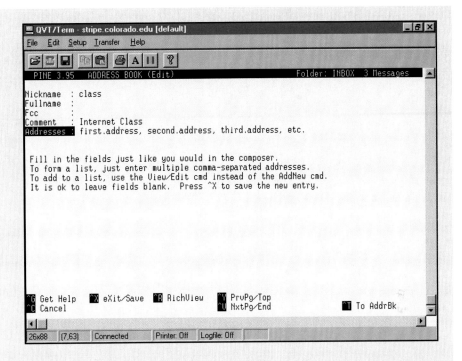

When you are finished, press Ctrl+X to exit your address book editor. To mail an e-mail message to everyone on the list, type **class** in the To: line when composing a message.

If you have completed your session, check with your instructor for further instructions; otherwise, continue with "Checking Your Skills" at the end of the project.

Checking Your Skills

True/False

For each of the following, check *T* or *F* to indicate whether the statement is true or false.

__T __F   **1.** An e-mail address can have a maximum of one space.

__T __F   **2.** All computers linked to the Internet run UNIX.

__T __F   **3.** To send and receive e-mail, you need to have an account on a computer directly tied into the Internet.

__T __F   **4.** An N preceding an e-mail message means that the message is new and that you haven't read it yet.

__T __F   **5.** You cannot change the subject heading in a message you are replying to.

Multiple Choice

Circle the letter of the correct answer for each of the following.

1. Press _____ to get online help while in the Pine main menu.

    a. Ⓗ

    b. ⑦

    c. Ⓐ

    d. Ctrl + Ⓗ

2. Which of the following can you *not* get from looking at your mail inbox?

    a. the size of the message

    b. who received a copy of the message

    c. who sent the message

    d. whether you are the primary recipient of the message

3. Which of the following is *not* a valid e-mail address?

    a. clarkd@bvsd.k12.co.us

    b. CLARKD@COLORADO.EDU

    c. david clark@mcp.com

    d. dclark@mcp.com

4. While viewing your inbox, which of the following functions can you perform?

    a. delete the message

    b. reply

    c. forward

    d. all of the above

5. Which of the following should *not* be included in your signature file?

    a. your e-mail address

    b. your street address

    c. a favorite quote

    d. your name

Completion

In the blank provided, write the correct answer for each of the following.

1. The e-mail address jsmith@utah.edu indicates that the user is from a(n) _____ institution.

2. To send a copy of an e-mail message to the printer, press _____.

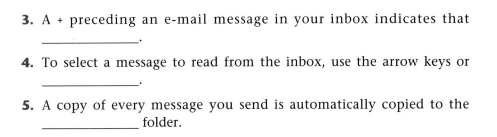

3. A + preceding an e-mail message in your inbox indicates that
_____.

4. To select a message to read from the inbox, use the arrow keys or
_____.

5. A copy of every message you send is automatically copied to the
_____ folder.

Applying Your Skills

Take a few minutes to practice the skills you have learned in this project by completing the "On Your Own" and "Brief Cases" exercises.

On Your Own

Creating an Address Book

Spend some time collecting e-mail addresses of friends and acquaintances. Put these addresses into your address book as described in Lesson 8. Spending some time doing this right at the beginning will save you a lot of time later on looking for addresses of people you want to correspond with.

To Create Your Address Book

1. Start Pine.

2. From the main menu, press Ⓐ.

3. Press Ⓐ again to make an addition to your address book.

4. Fill in the appropriate information.

5. Repeat this procedure as many times as necessary to fill in all the people you want to add.

Brief Cases

Sending Out a Mailing

One of your objectives is to keep your current customers aware of new releases. You collect e-mail addresses of regular customers and send out a periodic mailing to arouse their interest and keep them coming back.

Note: Sending out unwanted e-mail on the Internet is considered bad form. Make sure you include only those people on your list who want to be included.

To Send a Large Mailing

1. Collect e-mail addresses of those who want to be on your list. For the purposes of this exercise, you can use the following addresses:

   rsmith@mtv.com

   jonesm@usc.edu

   david433@aol.com

   oscar@ucab.al.us

   pitts@umaine.maine.edu

These are not real addresses; messages sent to these addresses will bounce back to you. If you want to substitute real addresses, feel free.

2. Start Pine.

3. From the main menu, press Ⓐ to enter your address book.

4. Press Ⓐ to start your list.

5. Follow the instructions in Lesson 8 to complete your list.

Project

3

Using Mailing Lists

Objectives

In this project you learn how to:

- Search for a Mailing List of Interest to You
- Subscribe to a LISTSERV
- Read Postings
- Post to a Mailing List
- Set the Digest Option
- Find Out Who Has Subscribed to the List
- Stop Mail Temporarily
- Unsubscribe to the List

Why Would I Do This?

A *mailing list* is a topic-oriented discussion group that uses e-mail as its means of communication. There are thousands of such lists based on just about any topic you can imagine. Subscribing to a mailing list can bring you into contact with other people all over the world who share your interests and passions. Mailing lists are great resources for learning about a given topic, finding research sources, and making new friends.

The three major types of mailing lists are LISTSERVs, Listprocs, and Majordomo. These mailing lists have a lot of similarities in the way they work. In fact, many of the commands are the same. The most common type of mailing list is a LISTSERV group. There are currently about 4,000 LISTSERV groups—something for almost everyone. In this project, you work with LISTSERV mailing lists.

Lesson 1: Searching for a Mailing List of Interest to You

In this lesson, you use Pine to search for a LISTSERV mailing list that focuses on a topic of personal interest. In addition to lists that can serve you professionally—such as lists for chemists, business people, and teachers—there are also mailing lists for just about any hobby or interest you can imagine. Bonsai, genealogy, and fly fishing are just a few of the offerings you will find.

To Search for a Mailing List

❶ Start Pine.

Pine is loaded and you see the main menu.

❷ Press Ⓒ to compose a new message.

❸ In the To: line, type the address LISTSERV@LISTSERV.NET.

❹ Leave the Subject: line blank.

❺ In the Message Text area, type LIST GLOBAL /[KEYWORD].

Replace *[KEYWORD]* with the name of the topic for which you are searching. Enter a topic that is of interest to you. Note that the commands are in uppercase letters. Generally, when dealing with LIST-SERV commands or e-mail addresses, they are not case-sensitive, but just to be on the safe side, always copy an address (or a UNIX command) exactly as you see it. A LISTSERV convention is to use all uppercase when sending commands. Figure 3.1 shows a search for chess-related topics.

6 **Delete your signature file.**

Figure 3.1
A search request for chess-related topics.

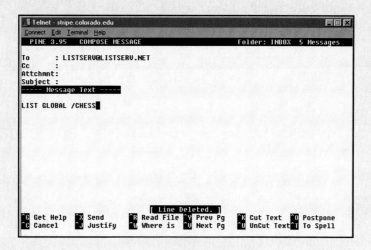

7 **Send the message by pressing Ctrl+X.**

Pine asks you to confirm that you want to send the message.

8 **Press Y.**

You are returned to your mail inbox. After several minutes, if your search was successful, you will receive two messages. Figure 3.2 shows an example of two messages received after a successful search.

Figure 3.2
Two messages received after a successful search.

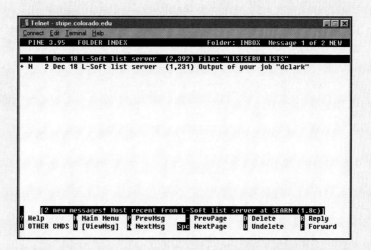

The second message has the subject heading Output of your job and tells you whether or not your search was successful. This message also lets you know how much computing energy it took to perform your search. If there are no lists matching your search criteria, this is the only message you will get.

continues

To Learn Parts of the Screen (continued)

A search for a LISTSERV of *donuts*, for example, returned the following message:

```
Date: Fri, 20 Dec 1996 16:13:16 +0100
From: "L-Soft list server at SEARN (1.8c)" <LISTSERV@SEARN.SUNET.SE>
To: dclark@STRIPE.COLORADO.EDU
Subject: Output of your job "dclark"

> LIST GLOBAL /DONUTS
No list matches your search string.
```

9 Select the second message and press Del.

This marks this message for deletion. There is no reason to keep this message around as it has no other pertinent information for the average user.

If you have problems...

If you receive a message telling you that no LISTSERVs were found on your topic, try broadening your search. For example, if nothing came back on a search for chess-related topics, you could try a search using the word *games*.

The subject heading of the first message is LISTSERV LISTS.

10 Select the first message by using your arrow keys; then press Enter.

The information you need for subscribing to the list is in this message. Figure 3.3 shows information regarding subscribing to topics relating to chess.

Figure 3.3
Information needed to subscribe to chess-related topics.

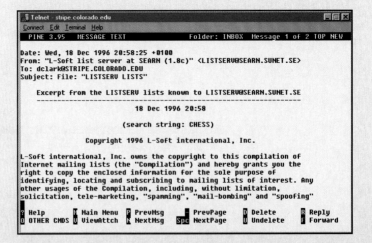

Now that you have the information you need, you subscribe to the list in Lesson 2.

You can omit the keyword in your initial message to LISTSERV@LISTSERV.NET and simply type **LIST GLOBAL**. You will receive a list of every LISTSERV known to this server. Beware, this file is very large.

You can also use the World Wide Web to search for a mailing list of interest. Use the following address:

http://www.nova.edu/Inter-Links/cgi-bin/lists

(In Project 6, you learn about these types of addresses.)

Lesson 2: Subscribing to a LISTSERV

Domain address

The address given to a computer connected to the Internet. The domain name of your host computer will usually be the last part of your e-mail address, after the @ sign.

After you have found a LISTSERV group to which you want to *subscribe*, you must send an e-mail message to the LISTSERV site address (not to the group itself), asking to subscribe to the list. This address is slightly different from the one to which you send your posting. The site address always begins with LISTSERV@ and is followed by a *domain address*, such as LISTSERV@LISTSERV.NET. A computer reads the e-mail message and decides what to do with it; your syntax and spelling must be correct.

Subscribing to a mailing list means that you agree to receive mail from the group. You will receive all mail posted to the mailing list. Any messages that you post to the list will be delivered into the mailboxes of all subscribers to the list. Depending on the list, this may be only a few postings or thousands.

To Subscribe to a LISTSERV

❶ From the Pine main menu, press Ⓒ to compose a new message.

You can do this with the LISTSERV LISTS message displayed on your screen or at any time within Pine.

❷ Fill in LISTSERV@LISTSERV.NET as the address.

Notice that this message is going to the LISTSERV site. Correct spelling and syntax are musts. For this example, you use CHESS-L as the group to subscribe to. If you have performed a different search and came up with a group to suit your interests, substitute the name of that group for CHESS-L.

❸ In the body of the message, enter the SUBSCRIBE command, the name of the list you want to subscribe to, and your name.

Figure 3.4 shows an example of a subscription request.

❹ Delete your signature file if you have one.

continues

To Subscribe to a LISTSERV (continued)

Figure 3.4
Example of a subscription request.

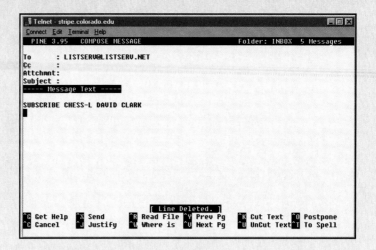

⑤ **Press** Ctrl+X.

This sends the message. In a short time, you should receive another message from the list management of your chosen list. Read this message because it often contains important information. Some lists require that a second confirmation message be sent to them before you are subscribed. Other lists simply send a welcome message. Depending on a number of factors, this may take several minutes or longer.

⑥ **Press** Q **to close Pine and return to your UNIX prompt.**

Some LISTSERVs are active with several postings each day. Others are slower. To ensure that you have some messages coming into your mailbox for the next lessons, subscribe to two or three groups by repeating the steps in Lessons 1 and 2.

If you are going to subscribe to a LISTSERV, you need to check your mail every day. Mailboxes can fill up quickly when you start subscribing to a number of LISTSERVs. Delete messages frequently and read only those messages with subject headings that are of interest to you.

Lesson 3: Reading Postings

When you join a LISTSERV, it is important to explore a bit at first, find out the tenor of the list, and get a feel for the people who post there. A new list can be a dangerous playground for a new user. Just as you wouldn't jump into the middle of a conversation without first finding out what people are talking about, you should also spend some time simply reading postings and find out what is going on. Many groups are very specific about what can and cannot be discussed using the list.

To Read Postings

❶ Start Pine and press Ⓘ to go into your folder index.

The messages that come from the LISTSERV will be mixed in with all your other e-mail. Sometimes, you can tell which messages came from which list by looking at the author column in your inbox. The subject headings in Figure 3.5 show you that there are messages from CHESS-L.

❷ Look for a posting from the list. Open the posting by selecting it with your arrow keys and pressing ⏎Enter.

Figure 3.5
The subject headings tell you that these messages are from CHESS-L.

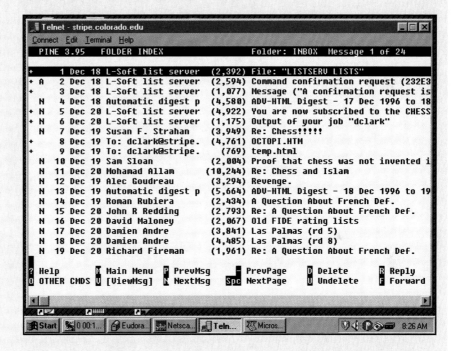

Read the message that appears on-screen. If the posting is of interest to you, you might want to create a folder to store postings from this list. This will give you a place to store items you find that are of interest for future reference. Refer to Lesson 5 in Project 2 to learn how to create a folder. If the posting elicits a response from you, you may want to reply. Replying is covered in the next lesson.

Lesson 4: Posting to a Mailing List

Posting
The act of sending a message to a list.

When you feel ready to make your first *posting* to a group, you send your message just as you would any other e-mail. The address to which you send the posting is different from the one you use to subscribe. The posting address is in the message that was sent back to you informing you that you are subscribed.

When you send off a piece of e-mail to a list for all subscribed members of the list to read, you are posting a message.

To Post to a Mailing List

❶ From the Pine main menu, press Ⓒ to compose a new message.

❷ In the To: line, enter the list address.

Use the address given to you in the initial posting. For example, the chess list address is CHESS-L@NIC.SURFNET.NL, as shown in Figure 3.6.

Figure 3.6
The CHESS-L list address.

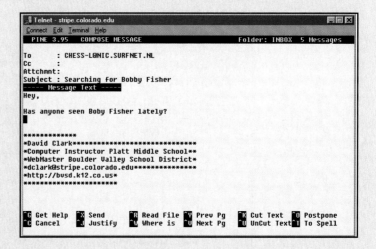

❸ Enter the subject heading.

Remember that this message is going out to people who get a great deal of mail, so make it interesting.

❹ Type your message.

If you have a topic in mind that you would like to raise with the group, write out your thoughts. If not, write a short note introducing yourself and stating your interest in the list.

❺ Press Ctrl+X.

This sends the message. When you want to reply to a posting made by somebody else in a mailing list, you have two options: reply to the LISTSERV or reply to the author of the posting. You can reply by pressing Ⓡ while reading the message you want to reply to. The original e-mail address of the author can be found in the mail header, as shown in Figure 3.7.

Be careful when making your first posting. Mailing lists are not places to practice your e-mail skills, and your posting should relate to the topic at hand.

Header

The information preceding the message body in an e-mail message. The subject heading, the date the message was sent, and who sent the message are just a few of the items contained in the header.

Figure 3.7
To send a personal reply to the author of the posting, not to the list, look in the header for the correct address.

author's address —

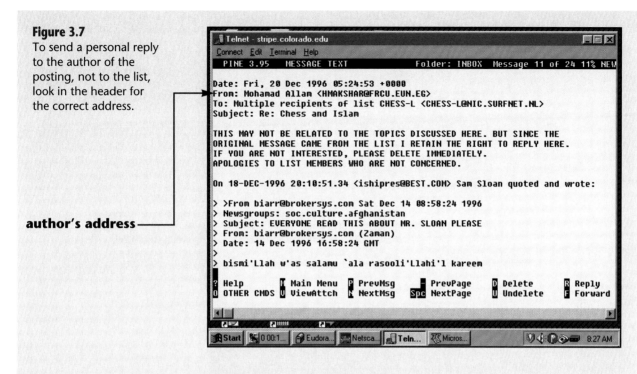

After you begin posting to the list, you will receive personalized replies from individuals. It is considered bad form to carry on lengthy conversations with one or two individuals using the list. If you want to communicate with an individual, use that person's personal e-mail address, not the list.

Lesson 5: Setting the Digest Option

Digest
A compilation of all the e-mail sent to a group each day.

To customize your LISTSERV subscription, you can set a number of different options. Setting the *digest* option is one way to customize your subscription. If you subscribe to a list that has a high volume of traffic, you may receive up to 100 e-mail messages each day. This amount of mail can clutter up your mailbox and create a tremendous clean-up chore for you each day. You can set the digest option so that all the postings of the day are rolled into one e-mail message. Instead of receiving 100 messages, you receive only one.

To Set the DIGEST Option

❶ Compose an e-mail message to the LISTSERV management address.

To find this address, substitute the word LISTSERV for the name of the list in the posting address. For example, in the CHESS-L@NIC.SURFNET.NL posting address, delete CHESS-L and replace it with LISTSERV. The address then becomes LISTSERV@NIC. SURFNET.NL.

continues

Your address will be different, depending on the LISTSERV you subscribed to.

❷ In the body of the message, type SET *[LISTNAME]* DIGEST.

Replace *[LISTNAME]* with the list name of the mailing list you have subscribed to.

Figure 3.8 shows an example of what your e-mail will look like when setting the DIGEST option.

Figure 3.8
Setting the digest option reduces the number of e-mail messages you receive.

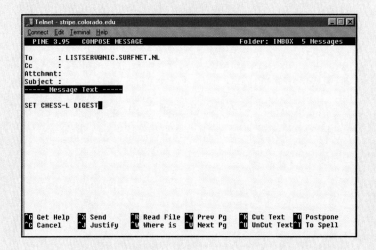

❸ Send the message.

Within moments, you should receive a message similar to the following, confirming your request:

Your subscription options have been successfully updated. Here are the exact settings now in use for your subscription. Please take a few moments to check that this is indeed what you wanted.

Subscription options for David Clark <dclark@stripe.colorado.edu>, list

CHESS-L: Ack=Yes, Mail=Digests, Files=Yes, Repro=No, Header=Full, Conceal=No

This message also provides additional information about some of the other options in the bottom line. From this point on, you will receive only periodic e-mail messages from this list rather than dozens or even hundreds.

Lesson 6: Finding Out Who Has Subscribed to the List

It is possible to find out about the other people who have subscribed to the list. Perhaps there is someone you already know on the list, or you just want to see how many other people have subscribed to it. You can easily find this information with the REVIEW command.

To Find Out Who Has Subscribed to the List

❶ From the Pine main menu, press Ⓒ.

You are going to compose an e-mail message to the LISTSERV management address. Remember, this address will begin with LIST-SERV@.

❷ In the body of the message, type REVIEW [LISTNAME], replacing [LISTNAME] with your mailing list name.

❸ Press Ctrl+Ⓧ.

This sends the message. Within moments, you will receive an e-mail with information about the list, including the names of the members and their e-mail addresses.

To hide your name from the REVIEW command, type **SET [LISTNAME] CONCEAL**.

Lesson 7: Stopping Mail Temporarily

Occasionally, you may want to stop receiving mail. Perhaps you are going on vacation, your computer needs to be taken in for repairs, or you don't have time to check your messages for a while. In such instances, you can unsubscribe to the list, as discussed in Lesson 8, and subscribe again when you are ready to receive messages. You can also use the nomail option.

If you have gone to the trouble of customizing your subscription, the NOMAIL option may be the best for you. If you unsubscribe, you will have to reset all your options when you are ready to be active on the Net again.

To Stop Mail Temporarily

❶ Compose a message to the LISTSERV address.

❷ In the body of the message, type SET [LISTNAME] NOMAIL.

❸ Send the message.

In a matter of minutes, you will receive a message confirming your actions. To receive mail again, send the request **SET [LISTNAME] mail**, replacing [LISTNAME] with your mailing list name.

All these options can be set with the following commands:

SET [LISTNAME] DIGEST

REVIEW [LISTNAME]

SET [LISTNAME] NOMAIL

You can set a number of other options to tweak your subscription to fit your needs. To find out more about these, send a request to the LISTSERV site. In the body, type **HELP** or **INFO REFCARD**.

Send the message. A reply will quickly find its way into your mailbox.

Lesson 8: Unsubscribing to the List

When it is time to say good-bye to the LISTSERV, you need to issue an UNSUBSCRIBE command.

To Unsubscribe to the Mailing List

❶ **Post a message to the LISTSERV management site.**

❷ **In the body, type UNSUBSCRIBE [LISTNAME].**

It is not necessary to include your name in the command. Figure 3.9 shows an example of the command to unsubscribe.

Figure 3.9
Signing off a LISTSERV.

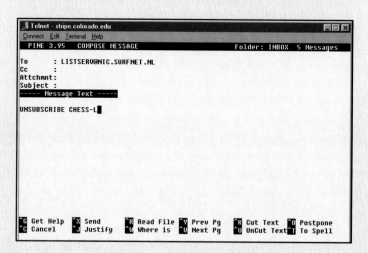

❸ **Send the message.**

Shortly, you will stop receiving e-mail from the list.

If you have completed your session on the computer, check with your instructor for further instructions; otherwise, continue with "Checking Your Skills" at the end of this project.

Checking Your Skills

True/False

For each of the following, check *T* or *F* to indicate whether the statement is true or false.

__T __F **1.** Commands sent to the LISTSERV management address go in the Subject: line.

__T __F **2.** You must erase your signature file when sending mail to the LISTSERV management address.

__T __F **3.** You must have an e-mail account to subscribe to a LISTSERV.

__T __F **4.** When unsubscribing to a LISTSERV, you must include your name with the UNSUBSCRIBE command.

__T __F **5.** You don't need to include a keyword when issuing the LIST GLOBAL command.

Multiple Choice

Circle the letter of the correct answer for each of the following.

1. You can get on-line help by sending which of the following commands?

   a. HELP

   b. help

   c. INFO REFCARD

   d. all of the above

2. Which of the following is *not* a valid LISTSERV management address?

   a. LISTSERV@LISTSERV.NET

   b. LISTSERV@NIC.SURFNET.NL

   c. LISTSERVE@VM1.NODAK.EDU

   d. LISTSERV@UCSBMV.NUCB.EDU

3. Which of the following LISTSERV options do you use to receive a single encapsulated piece of e-mail rather than dozens each day?

   a. NOMAIL

   b. REVIEW

   c. DIGEST

   d. NOACK

4. Which of the following addresses would be acceptable to send a SUBSCRIBE or UNSUBSCRIBE command to?

   a. LISTSERV@NM1.NODAK.EDU

   b. CHESS-L@NIC.SURFNET.EDU

   c. LISTSERVe@COMPUSERVE.COM

   d. all of the above

5. Which of the following statements is true regarding LISTSERVs?

   a. Messages from LISTSERVs are automatically filed in a different mailbox from the one for your regular mail.

   b. LISTSERVs can be used to exchange personal correspondence.

   c. All LISTSERVs are very active and will put from 10 to 100 pieces of mail in your mailbox each day.

   d. none of the above

Completion

In the blank provided, write the correct answer for each of the following statements.

1. To mail a subscription request, you need to include the SUBSCRIBE command, the list name, and _____.

2. All LISTSERV management addresses begin with the word _____.

3. If you want to suspend your subscription for a few days but don't want to unsubscribe, send the _____ command to the LISTSERV management.

4. To receive a copy of every LISTSERV known to LISTSERV@ LISTSERV.NET, send the command _____.

5. LISTSERV is one type of mailing list; the other two major types of lists are _____ and _____.

Applying Your Skills

Take a few minutes to practice the skills you have learned in this project by completing the "On Your Own" and "Brief Cases" exercises.

On Your Own

Getting the FAQs Straight

Many mailing lists maintain a *FAQ*, which stands for frequently asked questions. This is a text document that answers basic questions regarding the mission and netiquette (Net etiquette) of posting to the group. The FAQ is in a question-and-answer format and can provide you with good information as to the workings of a particular mailing list. It is a good idea to have this document before jumping into the discussion.

Finding the FAQ

1. Start your e-mail program.

2. Subscribe to a LISTSERV, if you haven't already.

3. Compose a message to the group (use the posting address here, not the LISTSERV management address) requesting information about whether a FAQ is available.

4. Send the message.

5. In a matter of minutes, hours, or days (depending on the activity level of the group), you will receive the requested information.

Brief Cases

Keeping Up with the Current Trends in Music

As the owner and business manager of Sound Byte Music, you need to know what is happening in the world of music outside the town you live in. What is hot? What is not? LISTSERVs can be an excellent way to collect information on current trends in the world of music and have the best inventory for the customers.

To Gather the Information You Need

1. Start your e-mail program.

2. Compose a message to LISTSERV@LISTSERV.NET.

3. In the body of the message, type the following:

LIST GLOBAL /MUSIC
LIST GLOBAL /JAZZ
LIST GLOBAL /CLASSICAL MUSIC

Include any other keywords you think might be appropriate.

4. Send the message.

Several mailing list addresses will be returned on music. Find one or two that look promising and send a subscription request.

As in previous examples, you will begin to receive mail from these lists. Once you have established an understanding of the group (either by reading the postings or locating the FAQ), you are ready to introduce yourself and join the discussion.

Project

4

Exploring UseNet

Objectives

In this project you learn how to:

Use a Newsreader

Use Pine to Access a Newsgroup

Choose Your Newsgroups

Post an Original Message

Post a Follow-Up Message

Unsubscribe from Newsgroups

Why Would I Do This?

Newgroups
Discussion groups in which people leave messages for others to read.

UseNet is a series of bulletin-board-like discussion groups, called *newsgroups*. Nearly 20,000 of these newsgroups on all conceivable subjects exist. Users with access can post to these newsgroups, and if they like, can respond to any of the discussions. Users can also suggest the formation of a new newsgroup. Newsgroups are created on computers all over the world.

Newsgroups can be used for business or pleasure. You can use them to spend time "talking" with other people who share your interests. You can even do some serious work online, such as finding a job, finding software, or researching a topic.

UseNet is a network of networks. It is not owned by anyone and is run by the people who use it. UseNet is simply a series of voluntary agreements to swap information. The most widely available newsgroups go through UseNet. UseNet is similar to mailing lists in that it facilitates the free flow of information on a given topic. The advantage to UseNet is that it doesn't clutter up your mailbox.

Understanding Newsgroup Naming Conventions

UseNet naming conventions may seem a bit confusing at first, but they start to make sense when you take a closer look at them. Newsgroup names look like host addresses: a series of words separated by periods. They are set up in a hierarchical system; the first name is the top level. Table 4.1 lists the top-level UseNet groups.

Table 4.1	Top-Level UseNet Groups
Group	Topic
comp	Computer-related subjects.
news	Information about newsgroups themselves, including software used to read newsgroup messages. This group also includes information about finding and using newsgroups.
rec	Recreational topics, such as music, hobbies, the arts, and skiing.
sci	Groups relating to the various disciplines of science.
soc	A wide range of social issues, such as different types of societies.
talk	Debate politics, religion, and anything else controversial.
misc	Everything else that doesn't fit into one of the other categories, such as job searches and items for sale.

Although these are the major categories, you will most certainly see others at your site. Some other groups are listed in Table 4.2.

Table 4.2	Additional UseNet Groups
Group	Topic
alt	Alternative subjects (often subjects that many people would consider inappropriate, pornographic, or just weird).
bionet	Biological subjects.
bit	A variety of newsgroups from the Bitnet network. Many of the LISTSERV mailing lists can be found in this category as well.
biz	Business subjects, including advertisements.
clari	Groups from Clarinet, which is a subscription service that brings information from the UPI and syndicated columns into newsgroups.
k12	Discussions about education in grades K through 12.

Lesson 1: Using a Newsreader

Newsreader

A program that helps you find your way through a newsgroup's messages.

Now that you know what newsgroups are, you need to know how to use them. News messages are stored in text files. The best way to read messages is to use a *newsreader* to help you sort through them. Several different programs can be used to read UseNet: nn, trn, and tin are a few of the programs you might find on your UNIX server. The commands to read and post to newsgroups differ from program to program.

In this lesson, you use Pine to read a newsgroup message. The same program you use to read your mail can be used to read newsgroups. This is an advantage because you don't have to learn a new program or interface; the commands are mostly the same. You need to configure Pine, however, to be able to read the news.

To Use a Newsreader

❶ From the Pine main menu, press Ⓢ.

This starts the setup.

❷ Press Ⓒ.

This accesses the configuration window, as shown in Figure 4.1.

continues

To Use a Newsreader (continued)

Figure 4.1
The Pine configuration
window.

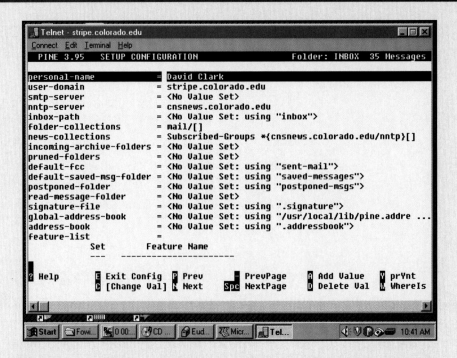

❸ **Use the arrow keys to highlight the news-collections option.**

❹ **Press Ⓐ.**

This action adds a value to the line. You are then prompted to enter the information.

❺ **Type the address of your news server.**

Get this information from your instructor or system administrator. The syntax must be exact, as in the following example:

```
Subscribed-Groups *{address_of_your_news server/nntp}[]
```

The asterisk at the beginning and the brackets at the end are important; don't leave them out.

❻ **Highlight the option nntp-server =.**

❼ **Press Ⓐ.**

This adds a value to the line.

❽ **Enter the address of your news server once again, this time without the parentheses and brackets; then press ⏎Enter.**

The configuration window also lets you customize your Pine session in many other ways. I would recommend looking for and checking the following item:

```
[X]  enable-suspend
```

This item enables you to return to the UNIX prompt by pressing Ⓒtrl+Ⓩ while in Pine. You can then return to Pine by typing **fg**.

❾ **Press Ⓔ.**

This exits you from the configuration. In order for Pine to read your new information, you must restart Pine.

Now that Pine is configured, take a look at which newsgroups are available. Each site carries different newsgroups, so your screen will appear slightly different from the ones shown here.

To Use Pine to Access a Newsgroup

❶ From the Pine main menu, press Ⓛ.

The Folder List window is displayed, as shown in Figure 4.2. Notice that the Pine screen now looks different from when Pine was configured to read only e-mail and not UseNet.

Figure 4.2
Working your way through Pine to get to the newsgroups.

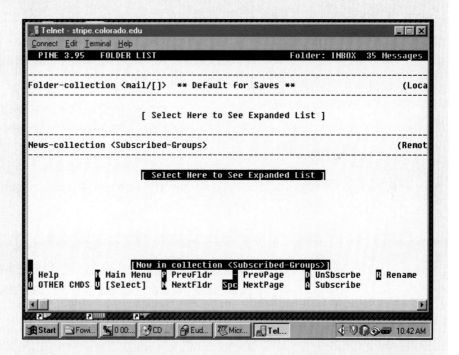

❷ Use the arrow keys to select the second option, Select Here to See Expanded List; then press ⏎Enter.

This takes you to the newsgroups.

❸ Press Spacebar to scroll through all the newsgroups.

The news.announce.newusers and news.newusers.questions newsgroups are created for new users only. These are good places to start.

❹ Press Ⓐ.

This action finds the newsgroups for new users. You are then prompted for the name of a newsgroup to which you want to subscribe.

continues

To Use Pine to Access a Newsgroup (continued)

5 Type news.newusers.questions as shown in Figure 4.3; then press ↵Enter twice.

Figure 4.3
Typing the name of the group you want to subscribe to.

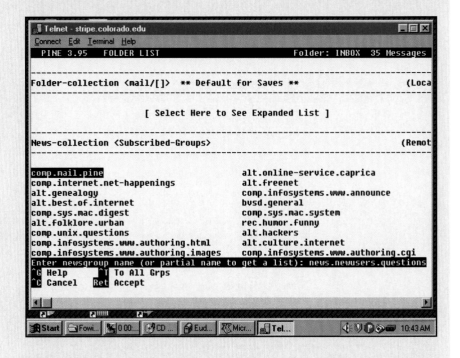

You then see a screen that looks similar to your mailbox (see Figure 4.4). *Warning:* This group has a lot of traffic and may take a minute or two to open.

Figure 4.4
29,084 messages waiting to be read.

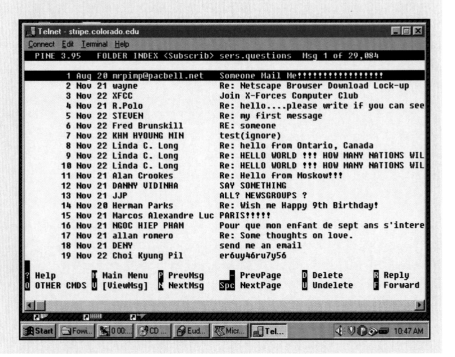

6 **Use the arrow keys to select a message and then press** ⏎Enter.

The message will appear on your screen. To return to the inbox to select a different message to read, press Ⓘ.

Depending on your site, you may have 2,000–15,000 different newsgroups you can read. That's more information than you could ever need. When you first enter the UseNet world, the computer has no idea what your interests are, and leaves it up to you to decide. In some cases, your school may have already created a customized list for you. In that case, you will be subscribed to 5–10 introductory groups.

Lesson 2: Choosing Your Newsgroups

To pick a newsgroup to which you want to subscribe, you can search through the list by using keywords. In this lesson, you use a keyword to choose a newsgroup.

To Choose a Newsgroup

1 **From the Pine main menu, press Ⓛ to go to the Folder List window.**

2 **Press Ⓐ to subscribe to a new newsgroup.**

This is the subscribe command. You then see the prompt `Enter newsgroup name (or partial name to get a list):`.

3 **Enter the keyword of interest to you.**

For example, to do a search for groups relating to Mexico, you would type **mexico**, as shown in Figure 4.5.

continues

To Choose a Newsgroup (continued)

Figure 4.5
Searching for news-
groups relating to
Mexico.

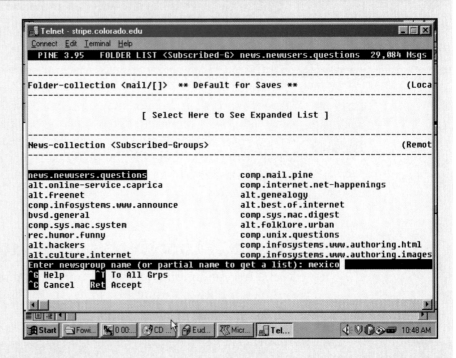

4 Press ⏎Enter.

A search is then performed for a keyword match, and a list of newsgroups relating to your keyword will be returned.

Figure 4.6
Newsgroups relating
to Mexico.

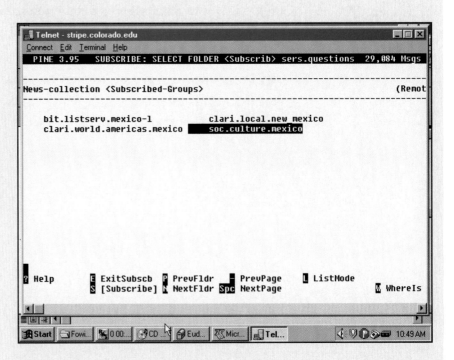

Note: Pressing ⏎Enter works only if you are using Pine 3.92 or later.
If you are using an earlier version, substitute Ctrl+X for ⏎Enter in
this step.

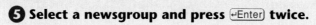

5 Select a newsgroup and press ⏎Enter twice.

You will then see the postings. Figure 4.7 shows postings from soc.culture.mexico.

Figure 4.7
Going to Mexico via USENET.

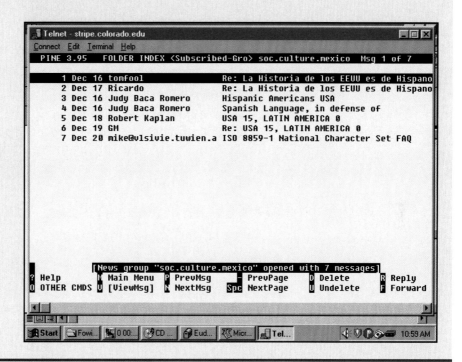

If you have problems...

If your search comes back empty, you can broaden your search parameters, or you can ask your system administrator whether any newsgroups are available on your topic. Most sites do not carry every newsgroup that is available.

Lesson 3: Posting an Original Message

An original posting is the start of a new discussion. You may want to ask for help on a particular topic relating to the newsgroup, offer a personal opinion, or share an anecdote. First, you need to decide on the newsgroup to which you want to post the message. In this lesson, you use the newsgroup news.newusers.questions to post a message.

To Post an Original Message

❶ From the Pine main menu, press Ⓛ.

❷ Open the newsgroup folders and press Ⓐ.

You are then prompted for the name of a newsgroup.

❸ Type news.newusers.questions and press ⏎Enter.

You enter the newsgroup for newusers.

As a newcomer to a newsgroup, you should get a feel for the group, read some postings, and get to know what is appropriate and what is not appropriate. One way of learning about a particular group is to read the FAQ. FAQs (frequently asked questions) were discussed in Project 3 in reference to mailing lists. FAQs also exist for newsgroups. As a first timer in a newsgroup, read the FAQ.

❹ Press Ⓒ.

Pine asks whether you want to post a message.

❺ Press Ⓨ.

This enables you to compose a new message.

❻ Enter the subject heading.

For example, type **FAQ?.**

❼ Enter your message as shown in Figure 4.8, just as if you were sending an e-mail through Pine.

Figure 4.8
Requesting the FAQ.

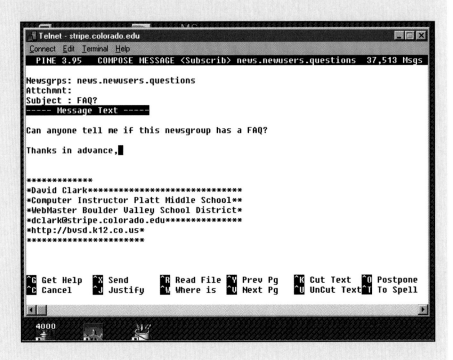

8 Press Ctrl+X and then press Y.

This sends the message. It takes a couple of hours for a posting to reach the newsgroup. When it does reach the newsgroup, expect to receive several replies.

Lesson 4: Posting a Follow-Up Message

A follow-up message is a reply made to the group to comment on a posting made by another subscriber. After reading through some newsgroups and finding a message that interests you, you can reply (or post) to it. You can identify a follow-up message by the reference Re: preceding the subject heading in the newsgroup list (see Figure 4.9).

Figure 4.9

Messages 4, 6, 10, 13, and 16 are follow-up postings.

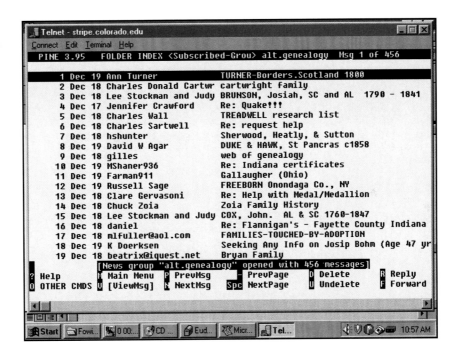

If you would like to follow the thread of an ongoing conversation, sort your mailbox by subject headings. This puts all the messages discussing a given topic together sequentially in your mailbox. Follow these steps:

1. Press $.

2. Press S.

Your messages will now be sorted by subject instead of date received.

To Post a Follow-Up Message

❶ **Open the newsgroup to which you want to post.**

❷ **Open the message you want to reply to, or select it from the Index.**

❸ **Press** Ⓕ.

You should now be in the Mail Editor, where you can compose a follow-up message. The address and subject will be filled in for you.

❹ **Compose your message.**

The cursor is placed in the Pine editor, and you can start typing.

❺ **Press** Ⓒtrl+Ⓧ **and then press** Ⓨ.

The message is sent.

If you want to send a reply to the author of a posting but not to the entire group, press Ⓡ. The address is automatically entered.

Lesson 5: Unsubscribing from Newsgroups

There is an advantage in unsubscribing to all the groups that you don't read: When you enter Pine to read your newsgroups, only those that are of interest to you are listed.

To Unsubscribe from a Newsgroup

❶ **Open the newsgroup folders in Pine.**

❷ **Use the arrow keys to select the newsgroup you want to unsubscribe from.**

❸ **Press** Ⓓ.

You are asked whether you really want to unsubscribe, as shown in Figure 4.10.

Figure 4.10
Unsubscribing from
rec.humor.funny.

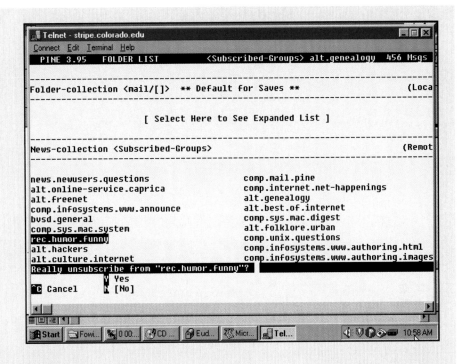

```
 Telnet - stripe.colorado.edu                              _ □ ☒
Connect  Edit  Terminal  Help
   PINE 3.95    FOLDER LIST        <Subscribed-Groups> alt.genealogy   456 Msgs
-----------------------------------------------------------------------------
Folder-collection <mail/[]>  ** Default for Saves **                    (Loca

-----------------------------------------------------------------------------
                  [ Select Here to See Expanded List ]

-----------------------------------------------------------------------------
News-collection <Subscribed-Groups>                                    (Remot
-----------------------------------------------------------------------------

news.newusers.questions              comp.mail.pine
alt.online-service.caprica           comp.internet.net-happenings
alt.freenet                          alt.genealogy
comp.infosystems.www.announce        alt.best.of.internet
bvsd.general                         comp.sys.mac.digest
comp.sys.mac.system                  alt.folklore.urban
rec.humor.funny                      comp.unix.questions
alt.hackers                          comp.infosystems.www.authoring.html
alt.culture.internet                 comp.infosystems.www.authoring.images
Really unsubscribe from "rec.humor.funny"?
                        Y Yes
 C Cancel              N [No]

 ◀ |                                                                    ▶ |
≣▣▣◀|                                                                    ▶
🅐 Start   📁Fowi... 📠0 00... 💿CD ... 📬Eud... 📺Micr... 📟Tel...    🔊 🕐 🌐 💾 10:58 AM
```

❹ Press Ⓨ.

The group disappears from your list. You can always subscribe to the newsgroup again.

Checking Your Skills

True/False

For each of the following, check *T* or *F* to indicate whether the statement is true or false.

__T __F **1.** Pine is the only program with which you can read the news.

__T __F **2.** It is considered bad etiquette to carry on a personal conversation using newsgroups.

__T __F **3.** Press Ⓢ to subscribe to a newsgroup in Pine.

__T __F **4.** When you subscribe to a newsgroup for the first time, it is best to read the existing postings for a while before you post your own.

__T __F **5.** After you read a posting in a newsgroup, it is possible to send a message to the author of the posting without sending the message to everyone subscribed to the newsgroup.

Multiple Choice

Circle the letter of the correct answer for each of the following.

1. Press _____ to unsubscribe from a newsgroup.

    a. Ctrl+U

    b. U

    c. D

    d. Ctrl+D

2. sci in a newsgroup name means that _____.

    a. the newsgroup discusses a topic related to science

    b. the newsgroups is reserved for scientists only

    c. the newsgroup discusses computer science

    d. both a and b

3. To get into the newsgroups from the Pine main menu, you must press _____.

    a. L

    b. S

    c. C

    d. A

4. A message posted to the newsgroup in response to a posting is called a(n) _____.

    a. original message

    b. follow-up message

    c. reply

    d. both b and c

5. _____ is another newsreading program that may be on your server.

    a. nn

    b. trn

    c. tin

    d. all of the above

Completion

In the blank provided, write the correct answer for each of the following statements.

1. Newsgroups that discuss Netnews generally begin with _____.

2. If a newsgroup name begins with soc, it means that the group discusses issues of _____ concern.

3. FAQ is an acronym for _____.

4. By checking the enable suspend option in your configuration, you will be able to _____.

5. The average site carries _____ newsgroups.

Applying Your Skills

Take a few minutes to practice the skills you have learned in this project by completing the "On Your Own" and "Brief Cases" exercises.

On Your Own

Keeping Your Fingers on the Heartbeat of the Net

Netnews can be a great tool for finding answers to difficult questions (the world is full of experts!), finding sources for information, and making important contacts. The newsgroup entitled news.lists discusses Netnews and periodically lists the top 40 newsgroups for the month. In this exercise, you find out where the hot discussions are taking place on the Net.

Searching the Top 40

1. Start Pine and press L to enter your folder lists. Press ↓ to access your newsgroup folders and then press ↵Enter.

2. Perform a search for news.lists. In case you have forgotten, press A to subscribe. When prompted for the newsgroup, type **news.lists**; then press ↵Enter twice.

3. Go through the messages and look for the list. You will know when you have found it by looking through the subject headings.

4. Read the list and find a newsgroup of interest to you.

5. Return to the newsgroup folders (press L) and perform a search to see whether that newsgroup is on your system.

Brief Cases

Keeping Your Fingers on the Heartbeat of the Markets

Just like LISTSERVs, newsgroups can be a great way to keep track of what is happening in the music world. As the owner of Sound Byte Music, you want to search for music groups and advertise the store to the rest of the music world. Many different music newsgroups exist. Filter out the groups that are not of interest to your business.

To Search Newsgroups

1. Start Pine.

2. Go into your newsgroup folders.

3. Perform a search using *music* as your keyword.

4. Use the option Subscribe to matching pattern (press Ctrl+X).

5. When the results are in, organize the newsgroups into the following categories:

   Music Education

   Computers and Music

   Musical Types (jazz, classical, and so on)

6. Decide which of these might best serve the interests of a small business owner. Subscribe to that newsgroup and start reading.

Project

5

Downloading Files Using FTP

Objectives

In this project you learn how to:

Make a Connection with a Remote FTP Site

Transfer a File into Your UNIX Directory

Download via a Direct Connection

Download via a Modem Connection

Decompress/Convert the Downloaded File

Why Would I Do This?

FTP
A utility used to transfer (upload or download) files on the Internet.

FTP, which stands for *File Transfer Protocol*, is one way to retrieve files from the Internet. (Using the World Wide Web is another way.) Many sites around the world have archived files on their computers and have made these files available to the public. The process of logging on to another computer to retrieve files is often referred to as "Anonymous FTP." The reason is that when you log on to one of these computers, you type **anonymous** as your login name and then give your e-mail address as your password. Using FTP, you can download these archived files to the hard drive of your desktop computer. Here are some examples of those files:

Shareware
Copyrighted computer programs made available on a trial basis. If you like the program and decide to use it, you are expected to pay a fee to the program's author. Sometimes called "try before you buy" software.

➤ *Shareware*, freeware, and public domain software

➤ Image and video files

➤ Sound and MIDI files

➤ FAQs and other text files

Lesson 1: Making a Connection with a Remote FTP Site

In this lesson, you make a connection with a remote FTP site and work your way through the directories. A rudimentary knowledge of UNIX is needed for this exercise. All the commands used here are explained in the UNIX appendix at the end of this book.

It is possible to FTP using a graphical interface over a direct connection (see the section that explains the procedure later in this project). In this tutorial, you use FTP via UNIX.

To Connect with a Remote FTP Site

❶ Log in to your Internet account and access the UNIX prompt.

❷ At your UNIX prompt, type ftp ftp.mcp.com **and press** ⏎Enter.

This tells the computer that you want to make a connection with an archive located at the address ftp.mcp.com, as shown in Figure 5.1. This connects you to an FTP archive at Macmillan Publishing.

Figure 5.1
Starting an FTP session.

After the connection is made, you are prompted for a login name.

③ Type anonymous as your login name and press ⏎Enter.

Next, you are prompted for a password (see Figure 5.2).

Figure 5.2
The prompt for your
password.

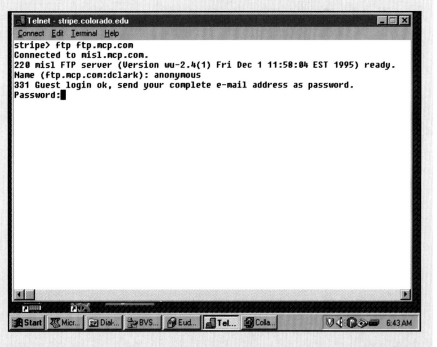

continues

To Connect with a Remote FTP Site (continued)

4 Type your complete e-mail address as your password and press ↵Enter.

Remember, a password does not appear as you type it.

You then see a message on-screen and a new prompt, `ftp>`, from which you will be working. From this prompt, you issue commands to move to the file you want.

5 Type ls and press ↵Enter.

ls is the UNIX command for listing the contents of a directory. You use this command now to see what is in the upper-level directory of this FTP server (see Figure 5.3). The dir command usually works here as well.

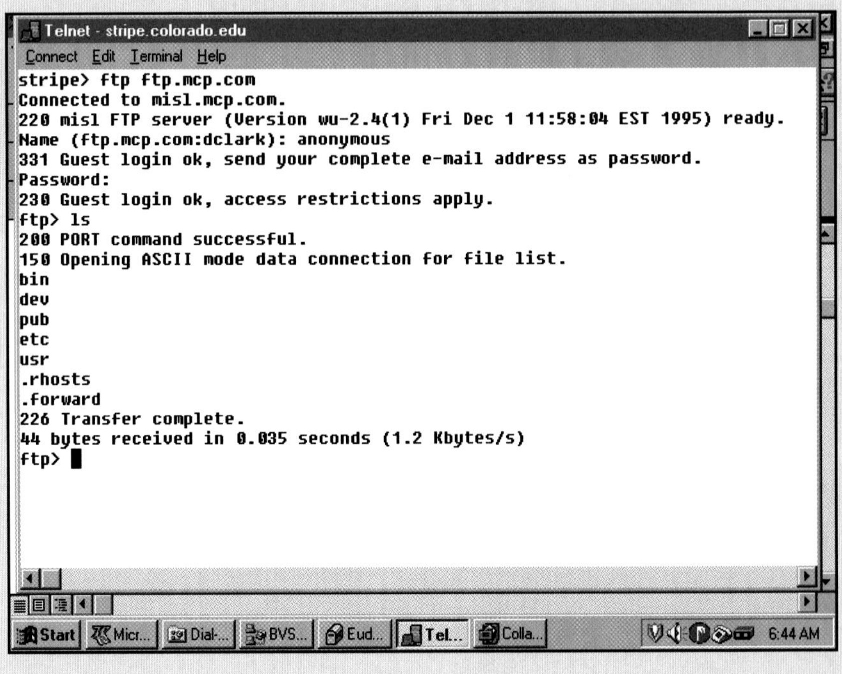
Telnet - stripe.colorado.edu
Connect Edit Terminal Help
stripe> ftp ftp.mcp.com
Connected to misl.mcp.com.
220 misl FTP server (Version wu-2.4(1) Fri Dec 1 11:58:04 EST 1995) ready.
Name (ftp.mcp.com:dclark): anonymous
331 Guest login ok, send your complete e-mail address as password.
Password:
230 Guest login ok, access restrictions apply.
ftp> ls
200 PORT command successful.
150 Opening ASCII mode data connection for file list.
bin
dev
pub
etc
usr
.rhosts
.forward
226 Transfer complete.
44 bytes received in 0.035 seconds (1.2 Kbytes/s)
ftp>
Start
Micr...
Dial-...
BVS...
Eud...
Tel...
Colla...
6:44 AM

Figure 5.3
The ls command lists the contents of the directory.

This upper-level directory contains the following five directories:

bin
dev
pub
etc
usr

FTP archive
Space set aside on a computer on the Internet and used for placing files for downloading.

Ignore anything preceded by a period. Most *FTP archives* have a directory entitled pub, which stands for public. This is the directory you want to explore now.

⑥ Type cd pub and press (↵Enter).

This command takes you into the pub directory.

⑦ To list the contents of the pub directory, type ls and press (↵Enter).

Notice the directory named software, which you access next (see Figure 5.4).

Figure 5.4
Making your way
through the UNIX
directories.

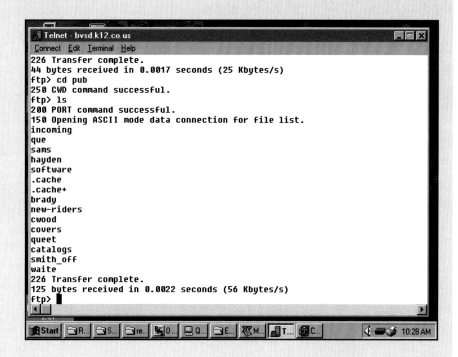

⑧ Type cd software and press (↵Enter).

⑨ To list the contents of the software directory, type ls and press (↵Enter).

Now search for a game to download.

⑩ Type cd games and press (↵Enter).

⑪ Type ls and press (↵Enter).

Figure 5.5 shows some files that you can download. You cannot always tell, however, which files are of interest. For example, with the file rgdaux.zip or immeen.zip, it may be very difficult to know what you are getting. Other files, such as mahjon.zip, are easier to decipher; the mahjon part of the file name shown in Figure 5.5 suggests that the file is the game mahjong. (You learn more about the .zip part later.)

continues

To Connect with a Remote FTP Site (continued)

Figure 5.5
A list of downloadable games.

```
Telnet - stripe.colorado.edu                                _ □ ×
Connect  Edit  Terminal  Help
doommd.txt
e-13sn.zip
epicba.zip
jill.zip
lbdemo.zip
mahjon.zip
overki.zip
rgdaux.zip
rgdmed.zip
simon.zip
wadtls.zip
zone66.zip
.cache
.cache+
dcnt12-1.zip
dcnt12-2.zip
rgde286s.zip
immeen.zip
xcomut20.zip
paddle.zip
decgb11.zip
tictactrivia.sit.hqx
226 Transfer complete.
527 bytes received in 0.033 seconds (16 Kbytes/s)
ftp>
```

In the next lesson, you learn how to transfer the mahjon.zip file into the UNIX directory on your host machine.

How can you tell whether you are looking at files or directories? Files usually have a file extension, such as .zip, .txt, .gif, or .hqx.

Often, you will see on-screen a file named 00INDEX, or something like it. This file contains detailed information about the listed files. To view this file online, you type **get 00INDEX |more** and press ⏎Enter.

Lesson 2: Transferring a File into Your UNIX Directory

Now that you have found a file to transfer, the next task is to bring mahjon.zip into your UNIX directory. First, you should know a little about file types.

ASCII
An acronym for American Standard Code for Information Interchange. A standard for computer-generated characters.

The file transfer can happen in one of two modes: binary or *ASCII*. You need to know what kind of file you are transferring. Table 5.1 lists some common file extensions and their associated file types.

Table 5.1 Common File Types	
File Extension	File Type
.zip	binary (DOS/Win)
.hqx	ASCII (Mac)
.cpt	binary (Mac)
.tar	binary (UNIX)
.gz	binary (UNIX)
.Z	binary (UNIX)
.txt	ASCII (any type)

To Transfer a File into Your UNIX Directory

❶ **Type binary and press** ⏎Enter.

Because mahjon.zip has a file extension of .zip, you know that it is a binary file and should be transferred in a binary mode.

❷ **Type get mahjon.zip and press** ⏎Enter.

This command, as shown in Figure 5.6, transfers the file to your UNIX directory.

Figure 5.6
Transferring the file via FTP.

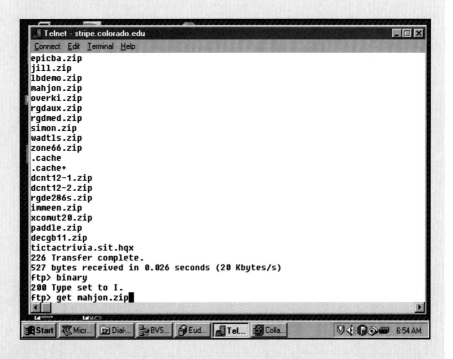

❸ **Type quit.**

This ends your FTP session and returns you to the UNIX prompt.

❹ **At the UNIX prompt, type ls and press** ⏎Enter.

You should now see mahjon.zip listed on-screen.

Now that you have transferred the file into your UNIX directory, you need to bring it onto your local hard drive so that you can use it. There are two different ways to do this, whether you connect to the Internet through a direct connection (PPP & SLIP are included in this category) or through a straight dial-up connection. Both ways are shown in the following exercises.

Lesson 3: Downloading via a Direct Connection

Downloading via a direct connection or SLIP/PPP dial-up account is easy. You can just point and click your way through the directories. Many good programs—such as Ws_FTP for Windows, CuteFTP for Windows, and Fetch for Macintosh—are available for transferring files. The advantage of using such a program is that the file is brought directly to your desktop computer, and you don't need to bother with knowing the UNIX commands. To use one of these utilities, you type, as part of the session name, the address you want to connect with. This lesson shows you how to transfer the file from ftp.mcp.com using Ws_FTP.

To Download via a Direct Connection

❶ **Locate the Ws_FTP icon on your hard drive, as shown in Figure 5.7, and double-click the icon.**

Figure 5.7
Opening the Ws_FTP program.

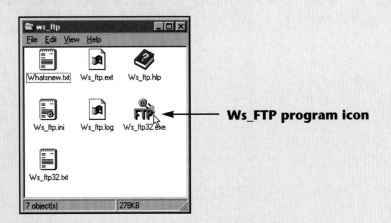

Ws_FTP program icon

A window entitled Session Profile is displayed.

❷ **In the Session Profile window, fill in the following information.**

Profile Name: Macmillan

Host Name: ftp.mcp.com

User ID: anonymous

Password: Your e-mail address

Leave all the other fields as they are (see Figure 5.8).

Figure 5.8
Connecting graphically
to Macmillan
Publishing.

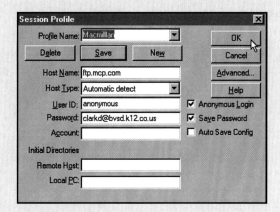

❸ Click OK.

You make the connection with Macmillan Publishing. Although the screen looks different, you have connected with the same FTP server that you connected with in Lesson 1.

The screen is split into two parts, as shown in Figure 5.9. The left side of the window represents your local hard drive. Notice that the path is D:\INTERNET\ws_FTP, which is the default directory to which a file will be transferred. Ws_FTP may show a different path to the default directory than the one shown in the figure.

The right side of the window represents the directories on the server at ftp.mcp.com. Notice that the list of directories is the same list that you saw in Lesson 1.

Figure 5.9
You are now ready to
move through the
directories.

Your local hard drive →

The directories on the server

continues

To Download via a Direct Connection (continued)

4 Double-click pub.

This takes you into the pub directory, and you should then see a new set of directories. Look for one called software. You may have to scroll down to find it.

5 Double-click the software directory.

This takes you into the software directory. Next look for the games directory.

6 Double-click games.

You have been moving through a series of UNIX directories by selecting the directory name with your mouse and clicking it. You are now in the games directory and ready to download the file. File names will appear in the lower-right window.

7 Scroll down until you find mahjon.zip, as shown in Figure 5.10, and double-click the name.

Figure 5.10
Double-clicking the file name to transfer the file to your local hard drive.

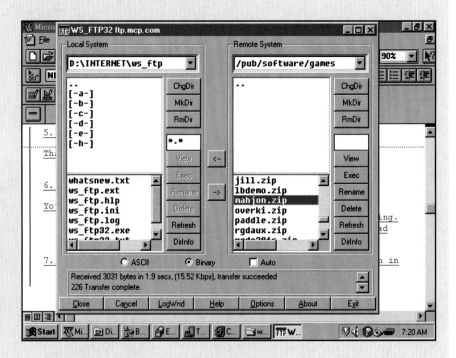

The file is transferred to your default directory.

Lesson 4: Downloading via a Modem Connection

After the file is in your UNIX directory, you need to transfer the file to your computer. If you are in a lab with a direct connection, you will want to use one of the FTP programs described previously. This lesson shows you how to download the file via a modem connection.

Protocol
A series of rules defining how computers react to one another when communicating.

Before starting this lesson, you need to know the transfer *protocol* that your communications software supports and the transfer protocol that your UNIX host supports. Three common downloading protocols are supported by many UNIX hosts: Zmodem, Kermit, and Xmodem.

For a number of reasons, Zmodem is the one to use. It is fast and has a recovery feature that enables you to resume an interrupted file transfer at the point of interruption. To find out what protocol is supported by your software, check with your instructor.

To find out what protocol is supported by your UNIX host, ask your instructor or system administrator, or type one of the following UNIX search commands:

> **which sz** (for Zmodem)
>
> **which sx** (for Xmodem)
>
> **which kermit** (for Kermit)

The UNIX command *which* is used to see whether these protocols are supported on your host machine. If you get a message indicating that the command cannot be found, you will know that your host does not support that protocol. For the following tutorial, you use the Zmodem protocol. Remember, this exercise will *only* work over a straight dial-up modem connection. If you are on a direct connection (or SLIP/PPP modem connection), the exercise will not work and will only freeze your connection.

To Download via a Modem Connection

❶ At the UNIX prompt, type sz -e mahjon.zip and press ⏎Enter.

Zmodem automatically starts downloading the file to your local hard drive. The download may take several minutes or more, depending on the speed of your modem. A 1-megabyte file will take approximately 10 minutes to transfer on a 14.4 modem.

❷ Once you have returned to your UNIX prompt, type exit to log off.

The file should be on your hard drive. Look for it there.

If you want to use the Kermit protocol to download the file, the sequence looks like the following:

```
bvsd.k12.co.us%kermit
kermit>send mahjon.zip
Return to your software and give a receive command
```

Notice that, after you type **kermit** at the prompt, it changes to kermit>. You then type **send <file.name> where you replace <file.name> with the name of the file you want to download** and press ⏎Enter. Kermit prompts you to issue a receive command. This command is in your communications software menu. Look for an entry similar to receive binary file.

The command to start an Xmodem transfer is the following:

```
sx -e mahjon.zip
```

Lesson 5: Decompressing/Converting the Downloaded File

Most binary files (such as programs, image files, and formatted text files) do not exist on the Net in a usable form. They are usually altered in some way to make the transfer of data quicker or smoother.

Most binary files that you encounter will be either compressed or converted to ASCII text. In a compressed file, the data is squeezed to create a smaller file for quicker transfer. This compression feature is appealing to users who pay by the hour for their connections. With a converted file, the binary information (the 01010101s of computer talk) is converted to ASCII text (to the characters and symbols you see on your keyboard, such as a, b, u, c, *, #, and so on).

PC users need to get a copy of Pkunzip or WinZip. These programs will decompress all files that end with the file extension .zip, which is the most common file extension you will see. Mac users need to get StuffIt Expander. These programs are available online and from user groups. Table 5.2 lists types of files you may encounter on the Internet, along with the decompression utilities needed for these files.

Table 5.2   File Types Encountered on the Internet

File Extension	Operating System	Decompression Utility Needed
.hqx, .cpt, .sit	Macintosh	StuffIt Expander
.zip	DOS	PkZip
.zip	Windows	WinZip
.arc	DOS	ARC
.gz	DOS or UNIX	Gzip
.tar	UNIX	tar
.Z	UNIX	compress

For this lesson, it is assumed that you have WinZip installed on your computer.

To Decompress/Convert the Downloaded File

❶ **Log out of the Internet by typing logout at the UNIX prompt.**

❷ **Quit your communications program and locate the downloaded file on your hard drive.**

❸ **From the File menu, choose New and then choose Folder.**

This creates a new folder in which you can expand the mahjon.zip file.

4 Rename the folder Mahjong by typing Mahjong and pressing ⏎Enter.

5 Transfer the mahjon.zip file to the Mahjong folder by dragging the mahjon.zip icon on top of the new folder.

Although this step is not necessary, it will help you maintain some sense of organization on your hard drive. If all the files are expanded in your default download folder, quite a mess will eventually develop.

6 Double-click the mahjon.zip icon.

If this is the first time you have expanded a .zip file on your hard drive, Windows 95 will ask you which application you want to use to expand the file. Otherwise WinZip will open and you will see a window such as in Figure 5.11.

Figure 5.11
Expanding the file using WinZip.

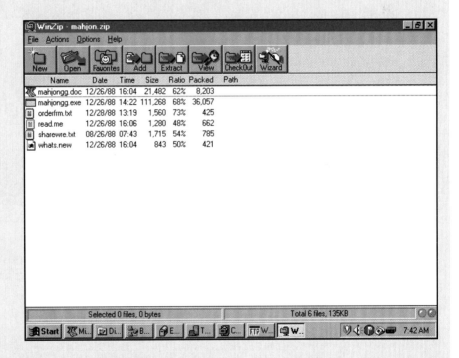

7 Search for WinZip in the list of applications provided by Windows and double-click it.

If it is not there, press the O**t**her button at the bottom of the window and navigate to where WinZip is on your hard drive.

8 From the Actions menu, choose Select All.

This marks all the files contained in the mahjon.zip file to be expanded.

continues

To Decompress/Convert the Downloaded File (continued)

❾ Click the Extract button.

You are asked where you want the expanded files to be located on your hard drive, as shown in Figure 5.12. If the default directory is not acceptable, navigate to a new directory.

Figure 5.12
Clicking Extract to expand your files.

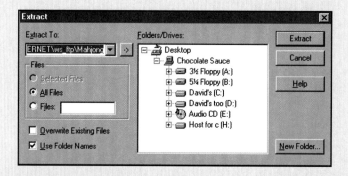

❿ Click Extract.

The file is expanded and ready for you to explore.

You will have to do this process only once. From now on, whenever you double-click any file with a .zip extension, WinZip will automatically load.

If you have completed your session on the computer, check with your instructor for further instructions; otherwise, continue with the "Checking Your Skills" section at the end of this project.

Shareware is not freeware. If you download a piece of shareware and decide to keep it, send in your shareware fees. They are usually quite reasonable, and the authors are deserving of your support.

Checking Your Skills

True/False

For each of the following statements, check *T* or *F* to indicate whether the statement is true or false.

__T __F **1.** When making a connection with an FTP server, use *anonymous* as your login name and use your e-mail address as your password.

__T __F **2.** When you use an FTP program over a direct connection, the file is first brought into your UNIX directory.

__T __F **3.** The UNIX command for listing the contents of a directory is ls.

__T __F **4.** All files must be transferred in binary mode to be usable on your local hard drive.

__T __F **5.** All files found on FTP servers will usually have a three-letter extension, such as .zip or .gif, to help you identify what kind of file it is.

Multiple Choice

Circle the letter of the correct answer for each of the following.

1. Which of the following is *not* a file name extension you will find on the Net?

    a. .zip

    b. .hqx

    c. .tty

    d. all of the above

2. Which of the following utilities are used to decode a file with the extension .hqx?

    a. Pkunzip

    b. StuffIt Expander

    c. Uncompress

    d. Gzip

3. You can use graphical interfaces over a dial-up connection with which of the following?

    a. SLIP

    b. Telnet

    c. PPP

    d. a and c

4. Which of the following is *not* a file transfer protocol that you would expect your communications software to support?

    a. Xmodem

    b. Zmodem

    c. Kermit

    d. pico

5. The command to connect with an FTP server at ftp.netscape.com is _____.

    a. telnet ftp.netscape.com

    b. ftp.netscape.com

    c. ftp ftp.netscape.com

    d. ftp netscape.com

Completion

In the blank provided, write the correct answer for each of the following statements.

1. Most binary files are usually _____ to make the transfer of data quicker or smoother.

2. If you download a piece of shareware and decide to keep it, you should _____.

3. The file dmfe.zip should be transferred using the _____ mode.

4. _____ is an example of an FTP program used over a direct connection.

5. Using FTP is one way of retrieving files; _____ is another other way.

Applying Your Skills

Take a few minutes to practice the skills you have learned in this project by completing the "On Your Own" and "Brief Cases" exercises.

On Your Own

Transferring Comet-Impact Images

Graphic images abound on the Internet. During the 1995 collision of the Shoemaker-Levy comet with Jupiter, images of the impact appeared on the Internet shortly after it happened. Those images and others can be downloaded. In this exercise, you transfer some images taken by the Hubble Space Telescope.

Transferring these images successfully to your hard drive doesn't mean that you will be able to view them immediately. To view the images, you need a graphics-viewing software package on your hard drive. Many good shareware packages are available via FTP.

To Transfer the Comet-Impact Images

1. At the UNIX prompt, type **ftp seds.lpl.arizona.edu** and press ⏎Enter.

2. Type **anonymous** as your login name and give your e-mail address as your password.

3. Work your way through the directories pub/images/comets until you come to the directory shown in Figure 5.13.

Figure 5.13
Image files of comets.

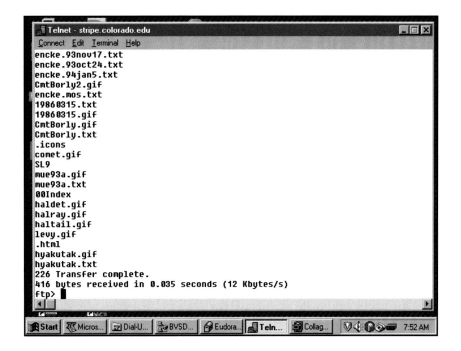

Any file ending with the file extension .gif is an image file. The files ending with .txt are text files and can be viewed online with the command **get file.name |more**.

.gif files are binary files and should be transferred in that mode. If you are in doubt about a file type, use binary mode.

4. Select an image file and transfer it to your UNIX directory by using the get command.

5. If you are connecting via a modem, use Zmodem, Kermit, or Xmodem to transfer the file from your UNIX directory to your local hard drive.

Brief Cases

Downloading Netscape off the Net

The latest version of the World Wide Web browser, Netscape, is available for downloading. In this exercise, you connect with the Netscape site and download a fully functional version. No respectable business would have access to the Net without having a powerful Web browser. Netscape is one of the best and will be used in the next three projects.

To Download the Latest Version of Netscape

1. At the UNIX prompt, type **ftp ftp.netscape.com**.

2. Type **anonymous** as your login name and give your e-mail address as your password.

3. Work through the following directories until you come to where the program resides:

pub/communicator/4.0/windows/

You can do this task in separate steps: type **cd pub** and press ⏎Enter⏎, type **cd communicator** and press ⏎Enter⏎, and so on. Or you can type a single command:

cd pub/communicator/4.0/windows

Substitute **cd 4.0/mac** if you are on a Mac. Note that this pathname will change as new versions of Netscape are released.

4. Transfer the appropriate file.

At the time of this writing, Netscape 3.01 was the current official release as shown in Figure 5.14; however, 4.0 was due for release soon and should be available for downloading by the time you are reading this.

There will be several different files and it is not always easy to know which one is right for you. Here is a rule of thumb, if you are using Windows 3.1, look for a file name with the number 16 in it (such as n16e301p.exe). This means that it is the 16-bit version and the right version for Windows 3.1 users. The Windows 95 version will contain the number 32, (such as n32e301p.exe) meaning this is the 32-bit file. The Mac version will end with the filename extension .hqx.

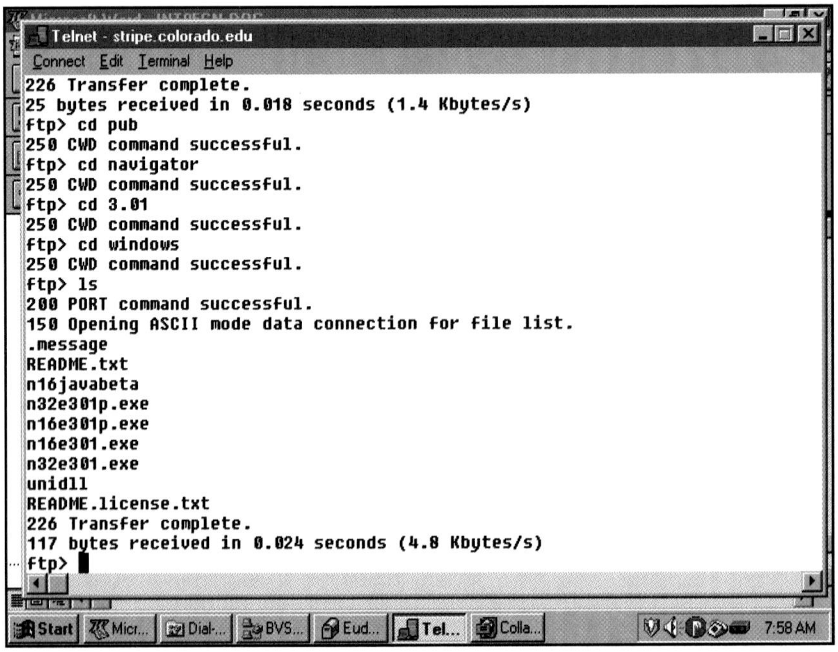

Figure 5.14
Netscape files.

When you find a file that looks interesting, use the get command to bring the file into your UNIX directory. Then bring the file onto your local hard drive by using Xmodem, Zmodem, or Kermit if you are connected via a straight dialup connection.

Another option to download this file is to connect directly to ftp.netscape.com using Ws_FTP or another FTP program to transfer the file to your hard drive as described in Lesson 3.

Here are a few other FTP sites you can try for practice:

mirrors.aol.com	Mirror sites for many Mac, DOS, and UNIX sites
wuarchive.wustl.edu	Lots of software, images, and graphics
rtfm.mit.edu	USENET FAQs in abundance
oak.oakland.edu	SimTel archive for DOS
archive.umich.edu	Great Mac site
ftp.ncsa.uiuc.edu	Home of Mosaic and other great software for accessing the Internet
quartz.rutgers.edu	Go here for a laugh
ftp.apple.com	Apple system software
ftp.microsoft.com	Updated Windows drivers, software, and Microsoft Internet Explorer

Project

6

Accessing the
World Wide Web

Objectives

In this project, you learn how to:

➤ Access the World Wide Web with the Netscape Browser

➤ Configure Netscape

➤ Navigate the World Wide Web Using Hyperlinks

➤ Download a File Using the Web

➤ Use Netscape to Read UseNet

Why Would I Do This?

etscape can handle many of the networking operations discussed in the previous projects with a single utility—a WWW browser. Using a WWW browser, you can do the following tasks:

➤ Easily find information on topics that interest you

➤ Download files more easily than with FTP

➤ Read newsgroups

➤ Send and receive e-mail

➤ Do keyword searches for topics of interest

Hyperlinks
A nonlinear link that connects a user to another site on the World Wide Web. These hyperlinks are represented as selectable pieces of text or graphics.

The structure of the World Wide Web is totally different from anything on the Internet. The WWW presents itself as a page of text with selectable *hyperlinks* to take you to resources on the Internet. These resources can include graphics, such as current weather satellite images; sounds, such as music clips; and full-motion video.

Lesson 1: Accessing the World Wide Web with the Netscape Browser

You can use many different browsers to navigate the World Wide Web. Netscape is considered one of the best. Netscape 3.01 is the current official release at the time of this writing, however Netscape 4.0, also called Netscape Communicator, is on the horizon and will be used for the examples in this project. Microsoft Internet Explorer and Mosaic are other browsers you will hear about. To run, they all require a dedicated connection or a SLIP/PPP dial-up account. Also available is a text-based browser called Lynx, which can be used with a straight dial-up connection. All the examples in this project use Netscape. A short section on Lynx is also included. If you are using a different browser, the configuration process will be different, but you connect to the Web in a similar manner.

To Access the World Wide Web with the Netscape Browser

❶ Double-click the Netscape icon, as shown in Figure 6.1.

This starts the Netscape application.

Netscape is initially configured to open to the Netscape home page, as shown in Figure 6.2. This page contains a number of great links to get you started. You will see several highlighted words (or words that are underlined or in a second color), which are links to other pages on the Web. Using your mouse, you can click any of these selections to make a different connection.

Figure 6.1
Double-click the
Netscape icon.

Netscape
program
icon

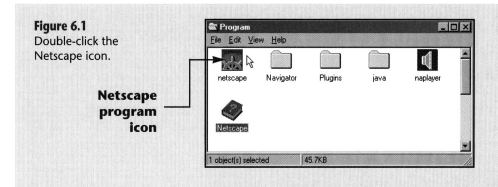

Figure 6.2
The Netscape home
page.

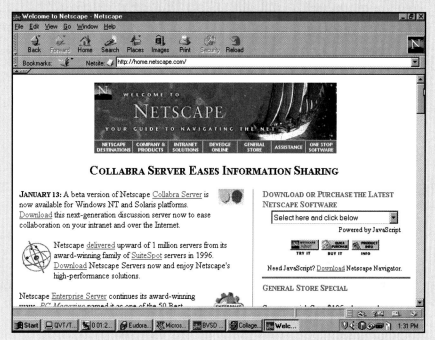

You may see a different page when you start up Netscape. The reason is that you can configure the program to open to a particular page, and the computer you are using is already configured differently. Here is an easy way to get to a place where you can start your explorations.

❷ Click the Places button in the Netscape toolbar and hold down the mouse button.

❸ Choose Destinations from the menu that appears.

Leave Netscape open for use in the next lesson.

Web Addressing

If you thought regular Internet addressing was confusing, wait until you get a look at a Web address. The good news is that you don't always need to know the exact address, because you can navigate with hyperlinks. You can select your destination by clicking or by selecting with the arrow keys, and the computer fills in the address for you. Even so, at times, you will want to connect directly.

Web addresses are known as URLs. URL stands for *Uniform Resource Locator.* A Web address looks like this:

http://bvsd.k12.co.us/schools/cent/Newspaper/ Newspaper.html

The http at the beginning tells you that you are connecting to a World Wide Web home page. http stands for *HyperText Transfer Protocol.* The rest of the information is the host, the directories, and the name of the file.

You can also connect with FTP servers through WWW browsing software. Here is an example of an address:

ftp://ftp.mcp.com

After you are connected, you can browse the FTP directory in much the same way you would browse any other resource on the Web.

Lesson 2: Configuring Netscape

The default Netscape configuration is enough to get you started exploring the World Wide Web. If you want to take full advantage of Netscape and the Web, however, you need to do some further configuring.

Note that, if you are working in a lab with a direct connection, many of these configurations may be set for you already. Parts of this lesson, therefore, may be unnecessary.

To Configure Netscape

❶ **Choose Preferences from the Edit menu and then choose Mail and News Preferences, as shown in Figure 6.3.**

The Preferences dialog box is displayed. You can set several options from this dialog box. To get you through the following lessons, you will be setting some of the basic options.

Figure 6.3
Using Preferences to configure Netscape.

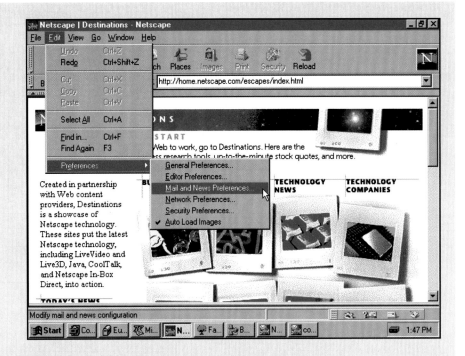

2 Click the Mail Server tab.

You now see a window like the one in Figure 6.4.

Figure 6.4
Many choices are available for configuring Netscape.

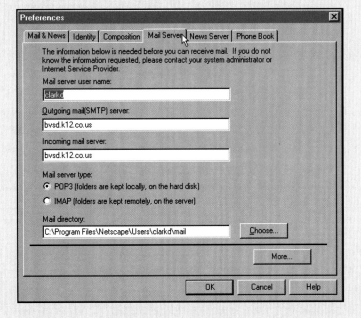

continues

To Configure Netscape (continued)

You use the Mail Server tab to tell Netscape your e-mail address, in case you want to send e-mail through the Web.

❸ Fill in the appropriate information pertaining to your account.

The most important items are your e-mail address and SMTP server address. Your e-mail address should be obvious. Your outgoing mail server and incoming mail server will most likely be the same—the host machine where your mail resides. This is usually the latter part of your e-mail address (everything after the @ sign). If you plan to use Netscape to receive e-mail, you can select a directory to store your mail.

❹ After filling in your information, click the News Server tab.

❺ Fill in the address of your news server.

If you don't know this address, ask your instructor or system administrator for that information.

❻ Select a directory where you will want to store any saved messages you may receive from reading UseNet via Netscape.

❼ Click OK.

As mentioned previously, you can set many other preferences from the **P**references menu, and you should take some time to explore those. For the next few lessons, the settings you have provided here are sufficient. Note, however, that if you are on a shared computer, such as a computer in a lab, you should erase your e-mail address from the Preferences settings when you leave. This is important. If you forget and leave your email address set in the preferences, any mail sent from that computer will look like it came from you.

Keep Netscape open for use in the next lesson, where you learn how to use Netscape to navigate the World Wide Web.

Connection, Hardware, and Software Requirements for Running Netscape and Other Graphical Browsers

If you are in a lab running Netscape, you can safely assume that all the requirements given here have been met. If you are wondering about accessing Netscape over a dial-up connection, the information you need is described in the following paragraphs.

You will require a direct dial-up connection like the one that a SLIP/PPP account can provide. Ask your system administrator about this connection. A new generation of UNIX software, the Internet Adapter, also makes Netscape available over a straight dial-up connection if SLIP/PPP is not available to you. You can find information on this software by sending e-mail to info@marketplace.com.

Here are the minimum requirements for hardware (for IBM compatibles and Macs):

    IBM-compatible computer (386 or higher)
    16M of RAM
    Plenty of free hard disk space (at least 10M)
    Windows 3.1 or higher
    VGA color monitor

Color Mac (LC or better)
System 7.0
Same memory and hard disk requirements as listed for IBM compatibles

In addition, you will need a 14400-BPS modem (or faster) if you will be accessing the WWW through a SLIP/PPP connection.

Your software requirements include Netscape or a comparable viewer, as well as TCP/IP software. For Windows 3.1, you will want to get Trumpet Winsock. Mac users need MacTCP or Open Transport, supplied with System 7.5, as well as a PPP package such as FreePPP. TCP software is also included with Windows 95.

Lesson 3: Navigating the World Wide Web Using Hyperlinks

The World Wide Web uses a series of hyperlinks to jump from one site to another. As noted, these links are highlighted on the Web page. To access one of the links, all you need to do is click it. This takes you to a new page and a new set of links from which you can choose. You continue clicking links until you come to the information you are seeking.

>

To Navigate the World Wide Web Using Hyperlinks

❶ In the Location box, just below the Netscape toolbar, type http://www.yahoo.com, **as shown in Figure 6.5.**

Note that once you start typing, the name of the location box changes to Go to:. Another name for this box that you will see is Netsite:. Don't be confused by the name changes, the purpose of the box remains the same—it is where you type in the address of the page you want to connect with.

Figure 6.5
Making a connection
with Yahoo!

Type the address
in the Location: box

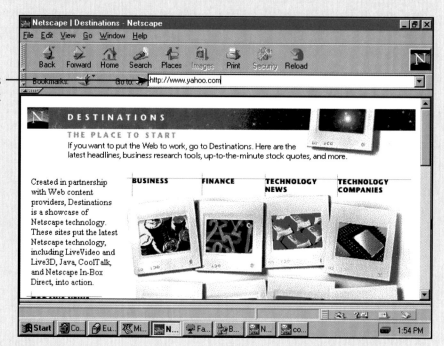
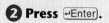

This connects you with Yahoo!, a popular place for Internet exploration. Its subject-oriented menu, searching utility, and depth of resources make it an excellent place to start.

❷ Press ⏎Enter.

If you have problems...

If you receive an error message telling you that the server is down, try connecting again. You will receive this message frequently when a server is busy.

At this point, you can start clicking buttons and following link after link. As Figure 6.6 shows, you can easily find something that interests you. Scroll down to discover more links, and then follow one of them to see whether you can find some information about current movies.

Figure 6.6
The Yahoo! page on the
World Wide Web.

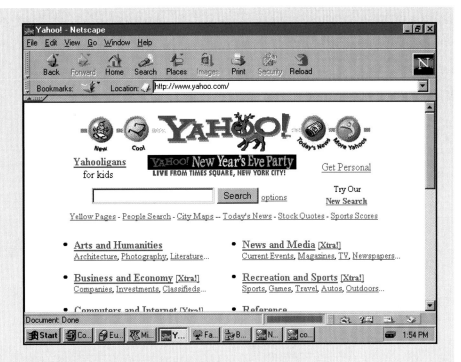

③ **Click Entertainment in the Yahoo! menu.**

④ **Continue clicking the following menu items:**

Movies and Films

Reviews

⑤ **From the menu on-screen, click one of the movies that looks interesting to you.**

⑥ **When you are finished, explore Yahoo! some more or choose Exit from the File menu to close the Netscape program.**

Lesson 4: Downloading a File Using the Web

You can use the Web to download files. If you are using Netscape, selecting a file brings it down to your local hard drive. Lynx drops the file into your UNIX home directory, and you then need to use your communications software to bring the file onto your computer.

Helper Application
A separate application automatically launched by Netscape to open a downloaded file, such as a compressed file, or to display or otherwise process that file.

When you use Netscape to access a file that includes sound and video, or to download a compressed piece of software, Netscape automatically launches the appropriate application to play or decompress that file. However, the first time you do this, you will have to show Netscape where this helper application resides on your hard drive.

Lynx—The ASCII Alternative

Lynx is a UNIX text-based browser for the Web. If you are dialing in from home, or if your lab supports only ASCII-based text, you will need to use Lynx. It isn't as pretty as Netscape or the other graphical browsers, but it gets the job done. If your host has Lynx installed, you simply type **lynx** at the UNIX prompt:

        stripe%**lynx**

If you know the exact address you want to connect to, you type the address after you type **lynx**, as in this example:

   lynx http://www.mcp.com

This connects you with the Macmillan USA Information SuperLibrary (see Figure 6.7).

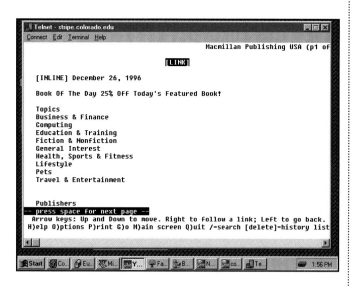

Figure 6.7
Using Lynx to access the Macmillan USA Information SuperLibrary.

You can move from link to link by using the arrow keys on your keyboard. If you want to explore a site, you simply select it and press ⏎Enter.

An important thing to notice on Web pages accessed with Lynx is a reference to an image, such as the following:

   [IMAGE] or [INLINE]

These references mean that a graphic is included as part of this page. Lynx will not display graphics.

Here are some other commands for navigating the Web with Lynx:

Command	Use
? or H	Displays a help screen
G	Goes to a user-specified URL or file
M	Returns to the main screen
P	Saves to a local file or mails a document back to you
Q	Quits
Z	Cancels a transfer in progress
A	Adds a link to a bookmark file
V	Views your bookmarks

For this tutorial, it is assumed that you have the appropriate software installed on your local hard drive. Table 6.1 lists different types of media and the software needed. All this software is shareware and available on the Internet.

Table 6.1 Common Multimedia Formats and Required Software		
File Extension	Type of File	Software Needed
.jpeg/.jpg .gif/.tga	Graphics	Paintshop Pro (Windows) JpegView (Mac)
.au/.snd .voc/.wav	Sound	Netscape Player (Windows) Sound Machine (Mac)
.mpeg/.mov	Video	MPEG Player (Windows) Sparkle (Mac)

To Download a File Using the Web

❶ Start Netscape.

❷ Type `http://www.shareware.com` **in the Location box.**

❸ Press ⏎Enter.

Netscape then makes a connection with this popular shareware archive (see Figure 6.8). One advantage to this site is that it enables you to search for a piece of software based on a keyword you type. Now do a search for the latest virus protection.

Note: All the media software mentioned in Table 6.1 can also be retrieved using this site.

Figure 6.8
www.shareware.com.

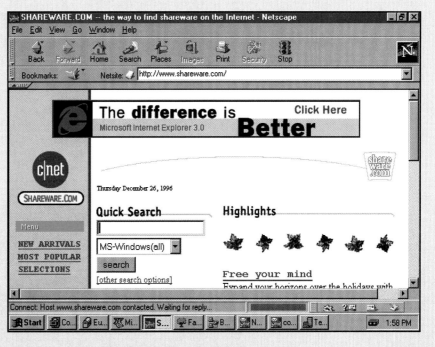

continues

To Download a File Using the Web (continued)

If you have problems...

This particular site is rather graphics-intensive, which means that over a slow modem connection, it may take a while to load. You can instruct Netscape not to load the graphics at all. Select Preferences from the **E**dit menu. **A**uto Load Images will have a check after it, select it and let up on the mouse button. This will turn off the Auto Load Images option. If you wish to see the images after the page has loaded, click on the Images button in the Netscape toolbar, the images will appear.

❹ **Type the word** `virus` **in the Quick Search box, as shown in Figure 6.9.**

If you are using an operating system other than Windows, click the selection MS-Windows(all). A menu will appear, from which you can select your operating system.

Figure 6.9
Typing a keyword to search for.

❺ **Click the search button.**

A variety of links will be returned. Scroll through these to find a file that fits your needs. For this lesson, you download McAfee's VirusSCAN for Windows 95, with the file name v95i206e.zip.

The .zip tells you that this is a compressed file. It will need to be expanded using Pkunzip or another compatible decompression utility after you download it.

6 **Click the link v95i206e.zip.**

Because this file is continually being updated, the file name may be slightly different.

www.shareware.com presents a variety of links from which you can download the selected file.

7 **Select one of these links (see Figure 6.10).**

Figure 6.10
Selecting the file you want by clicking on it.

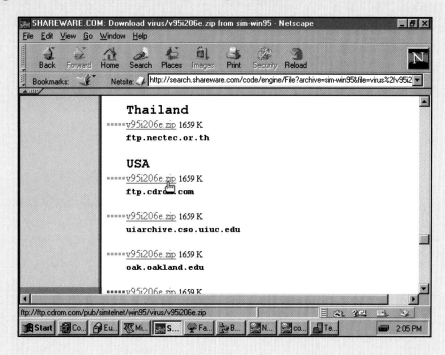

The file transfer begins. Windows then asks you what you want to do with this file.

8 **From the window that appears, click Save and use your mouse to navigate to the location on your disk where you want the file saved.**

Lesson 5: Reading Netnews Using Netscape

If you correctly configured Netscape in Lesson 2, reading the news is as easy as pushing a button. This lesson shows you how to read UseNet.

Using Netscape to Read UseNet

1 **Start Netscape if it is not already open.**

2 **From the Window menu, choose Discussions.**

Figure 6.11 shows the information that appears. From this window, you can receive and send e-mail and access UseNet.

continues

Using Netscape to Read UseNet (continued)

Figure 6.11
The World Wide Web of news.

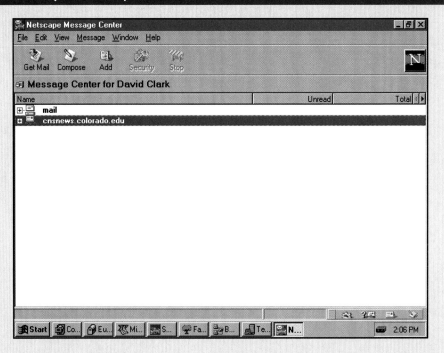

You should see the name of your news server listed, which will be different than that shown in Figure 6.11.

❸ Select Choose Newsgroup from the File menu.

A listing of the major newsgroup categories, as described in Project 4, will appear in a new window. Click the plus sign (+) next to one of them to view the newsgroups in that category (or in a subcategory of newsgroups). You may have to open more folders to find the newsgroup you are looking for. You can tell a subcategory from an actual newsgroup because a subcategory will be denoted by a folder icon and have a plus sign next to it.

❹ Once you have found a newsgroup of interest, click once on the newsgroup name to select it, and then click the Subscribe button, as shown in Figure 6.12.

You can now subscribe to other groups or click OK to return to the previous window.

❺ Click the plus sign next to your server name.

The newsgroup(s) you just subscribed to appears.

❻ Double-click the name of the newsgroup.

The postings then appear.

Figure 6.12
Click the Subscribe
button to subscribe
to a newsgroup.

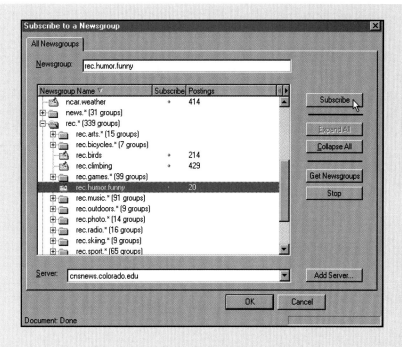

Figure 6.12
Click the Subscribe
button to subscribe
to a newsgroup.

7 **To read a posting, double-click it.**

The posting appears in a new window (see Figure 6.13).

Figure 6.13
A posting from
rec.humor.funny.

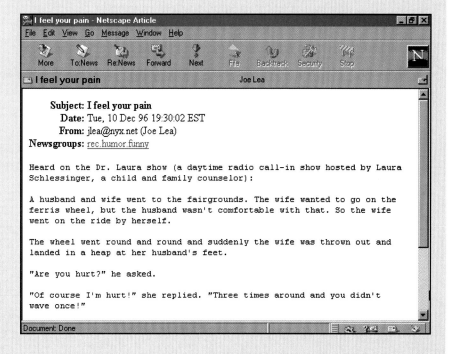

If you have completed your session on the computer, exit Netscape
and check with your instructor for further instructions. Otherwise,
continue with the "Checking Your Skills" section at the end of this
project.

Using the toolbar, you can post a message of your own, reply to the news-group, or mark the group as *read* so that you don't see the same messages over and over again.

Checking Your Skills

True/False

For each of the following statements, check *T* or *F* to indicate whether the statement is true or false.

__T __F   **1.** Netscape will run on any machine with the proper connection.

__T __F   **2.** The World Wide Web has a hierarchical system of menus that takes you deeper and deeper into the Web.

__T __F   **3.** All Web browsers display graphics, sound, and video files.

__T __F   **4.** A file name with the .mpeg extension indicates that the file is a video clip.

__T __F   **5.** Netscape is synonymous with the World Wide Web.

Multiple Choice

Circle the letter of the correct answer for each of the following.

1. Which of the following file extensions indicates a sound file?

   a. .zip

   b. .au

   c. .jpg

   d. .mpeg

2. Which of the following Internet functions *cannot* be achieved using Netscape?

   a. reading Netnews

   b. downloading files using FTP

   c. receiving electronic mail

   d. all of these can be achieved

3. Which of the following is *not* a valid address used in Netscape?

   a. http://www.mcp.com

   b. ftp://oak.oakland.edu

   c. http:/bvsd.k12.co.us

   d. http//:www.colorado.edu

4. Which of the following selections should you choose from the Windows Menu to read UseNet using Netscape.

   a. Discussions

   b. UseNet

   c. Folders

   d. Composer

5. The name of your news server can be set in which of the following Netscape menus?

   a. **W**indow

   b. **G**o

   c. **E**dit

   d. **V**iew

Completion

In the blank provided, write the correct answer for each of the following statements.

1. The World Wide Web uses a series of _____ to navigate the Internet.

2. _____ is the name of a UNIX-based Web browser that displays ASCII characters only.

3. http stands for _____.

4. For the dial-up user, Netscape requires a(n) _____ connection.

5. You can identify a hyperlink on a Web page because it is _____.

Applying Your Skills

The Web is where all the creative stuff on the Internet happens. Take a few minutes to practice the skills you have learned in this project by completing the "On Your Own" and "Brief Cases" exercises.

On Your Own

Finding the Newest and the Latest

New home pages are put up daily by businesses, schools, and individuals. You can see the newest and latest pages by simply connecting with the What's New? and What's Cool? pages.

To Connect with What's New? and What's Cool?

1. Start Netscape.

2. Click the Places button and hold down the mouse button. From the menu that appears, choose What's New?

You are presented with a selection of the newest pages on the Net. You can also browse the previous months' new pages.

After you see what's new, check out the What's Cool? page.

3. Click the Places button and, this time, select the What's Cool? option.

Again, you are presented with a wide selection of connections just waiting to be made.

Brief Cases

Imagine a computer set up at your site where customers can sample the latest music news or view the latest Billboard charts through the World Wide Web. You just need to know two words and one address, Billboard Online and http://www.billboard.com/. It's possible and easy to set up.

To Connect with Billboard Online

1. Start Netscape.

2. Type the following address in the Location box and press ⏎Enter

   http://www.billboard.com/

You are connected with Billboard Online, as shown in Figure 6.14.

Figure 6.14
Music abounds on the Web.

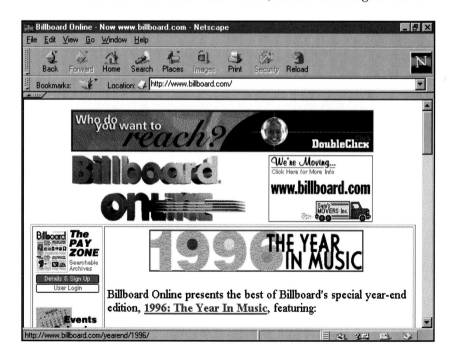

Note that this is a commercial service. You can visit several areas free of charge, but if you want more information than that, you will have to pay for using this service. Some of the information found here can be found for free at other sites, but you may have to do some digging. Select the Music link in Yahoo! for more music-related sites.

Project

7

Searching the World Wide Web

Objectives

In this project you learn how to:

Access the WWW Search Engines

Define Your Search Parameters

Refine Your Search

Save, Print, or E-Mail the Information You Found

Set a Bookmark

Why Would I Do This?

Being able to search the World Wide Web for a topic of interest has, more than anything else, made the Internet an accessible and useful tool for the millions of people who use it. Many good search engines have been created in the past couple of years. These enable you to type a keyword of interest, press ⏎Enter, and within seconds, dozens—sometimes hundreds or even thousands—of links are presented on the screen for you to follow in exploring your area of interest. This project shows you how to access those searching tools and how to formulate a query to help you find what you are looking for with efficiency.

Lesson 1: Accessing the WWW Search Engines

Without a good search engine, the World Wide Web would be nothing more than an incomprehensible jumble of information, and finding what you need could take all day or even longer. Fortunately, several good search engines can help. These search engines provide a variety of hyperlinks for you to follow. In this lesson, you learn how to access these search tools.

To Access the WWW Search Engines

1 Start Netscape.

2 Click the Search button on the toolbar.

From the window that appears, you can access several different search engines. Each engine has the potential to bring back page after page of hyperlinks on a topic. Take a look at one of the search engines now.

3 Scroll to the middle of the page and click the Yahoo! link.

This connects you with the Yahoo! search engine. There is also a Yahoo! link at the top of the page. Do not use that for this exercise; rather, look for the Yahoo! link farther down the page.

4 Type a keyword of your choice in the Yahoo! query box and press ⏎Enter.

Alternatively, you can click the Search button.

Yahoo! returns a page of links with information pertaining to the keyword you entered. Yahoo! searches the World Wide Web to find this information. In Figure 7.1, the topic entered in the query box is `endangered species`. This search for information returned 81 links for information on that topic and displayed the first 20 for viewing.

Figure 7.1
Searching the Net is as easy as pushing a button.

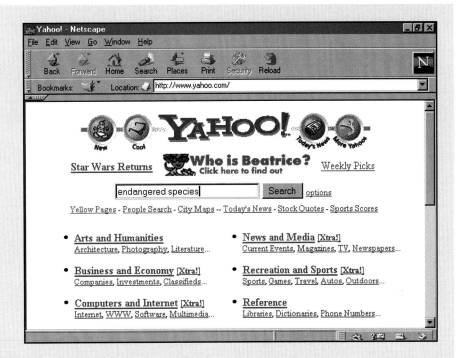

If you want a broader search, continue with step 5.

⑤ Click the Back button on the toolbar.

You are returned to the search page.

⑥ Click the options link next to the Search button.

Various new options appear that enable you to customize your search parameters.

⑦ Click the Usenet radio button and fill in the words endangered species, as shown in Figure 7.2; then click the Search button again.

Compare the information you receive with what you found in the earlier steps.

continues

To Access the WWW Search Engines (continued)

Figure 7.2
Searching Usenet.

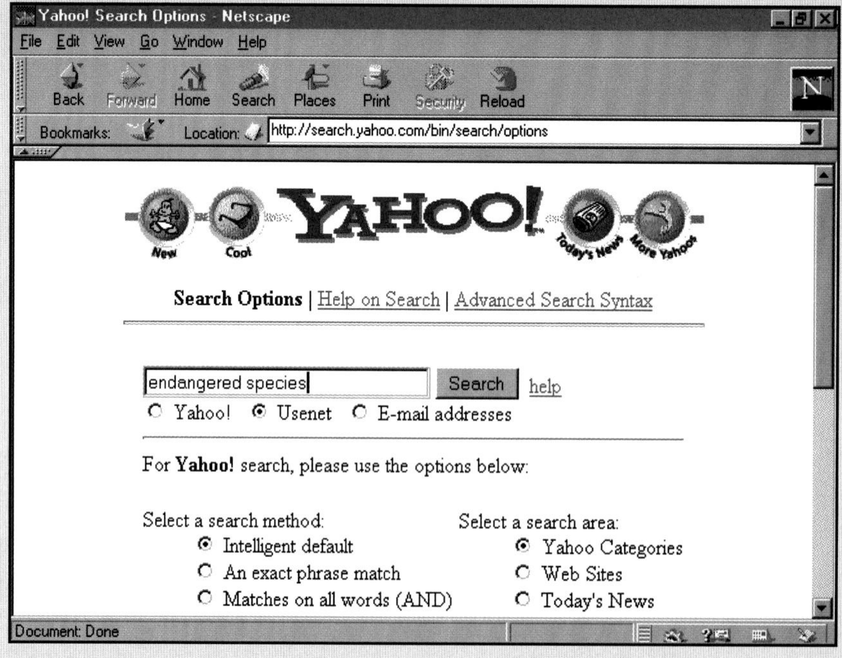

❽ **Click the Home button on the toolbar to return to your default home page.**

IN SIDE Stuff

You can also connect with Yahoo! by connecting directly to its URL. Use the following address:

> http://www.yahoo.com

Lesson 2: Defining Your Search Parameters

Sometimes you will want to perform a very specific search. With many of the search engines, you can get very specific on the topic you are searching. In this lesson, you look at the Open Text search engine. Open Text gives you the option to set some specific parameters for your search and to refine your search results.

To Define Your Search Parameters

❶ **Click the Search button in the Netscape toolbar.**

❷ **Scroll down until you see Other Services.**

❸ **Click Open Text Index.**

> This takes you to the Open Text search page (see Figure 7.3). Open Text gives you the option of performing a simple search similar to a Yahoo! search. You type a keyword and press ↵Enter).

Figure 7.3
The Open Text search engine.

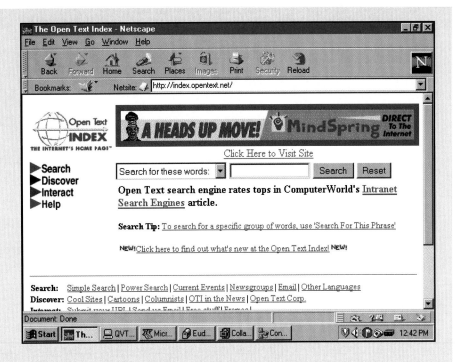

❹ **Click the Power Search link on the Search line near the bottom of the page.**

Open Text enables you to perform a "power search" in which you may use a variety of keywords joined by various operators such as AND, OR, and NOT. You can use these operators to more closely define your search parameters. These options appear as shown in Figure 7.4.

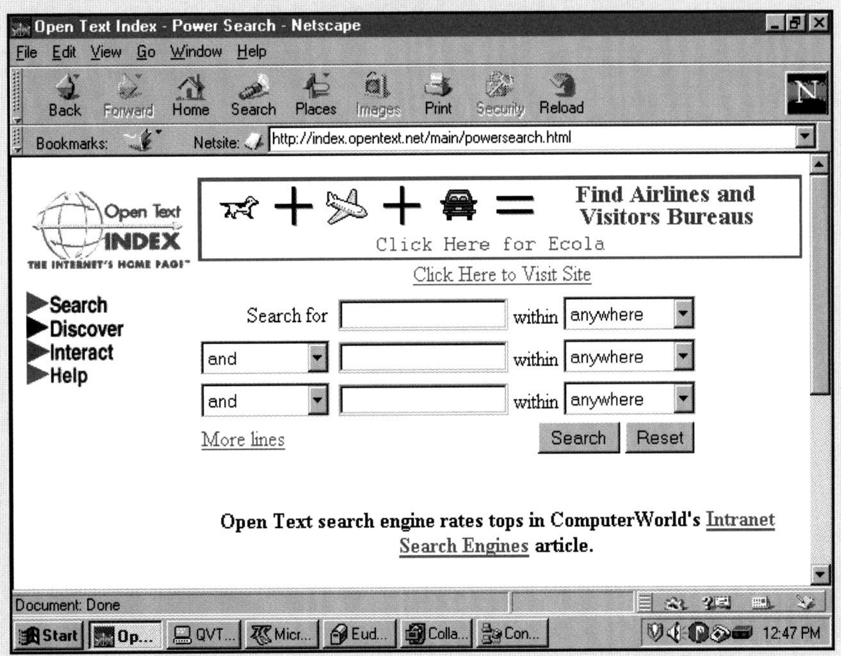

Figure 7.4
Additional search options using Open Text.

continues

This type of search engine uses a series of drop-down menus that help you customize your search parameters. The drop-down menus on the right (that currently say anywhere) let you determine where on a given Web Page you want Open Text to search for your word. Suppose that you want to do a very specific search for raptors on the endangered species list. Here is one way to do it.

❺ Click the top two drop-down menus on the right and select title; **leave the bottom menu as it is.**

This tells Open Text that you want it to search *only* the titles of Web pages and not the text that would be contained in the page.

❻ Type the word endangered in the Search for text box at the top, the word species in the middle text box, and the word raptor in the bottom text box.

The drop-down menus on the left let you assign operators to define the relationship of your keywords.

❼ Select the drop-down menu on the left (next to the word species**) and then select** followed by **from the options presented. Leave the bottom left box as it is, displaying the word and.**

Your search window should now look like Figure 7.5.

Figure 7.5
Narrowing your search
parameters.

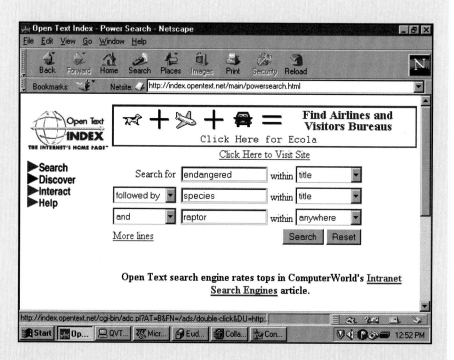

The parameters you have set for this search are the following:

Search for Web pages that have the word *endangered* followed by the word *species* in the title, and the word *raptor* anywhere else on the Web page.

8 **Click the Search button.**

You should be presented with several options of pages to view that provide you with information on your topic.

9 **Once you have finished examining these links, click the Home button to return to your default home page.**

Open Text can also be found by connecting to the following:

http://index.opentext.net/

Lesson 3: Refining Your Search

With some search engines, you can refine your search parameters even further. You can add extra keywords once your search has been completed. For instance, if you want information relating specifically to peregrine falcons, you could first perform the search as described in the preceding lesson and then add the words *peregrine falcon*. In this lesson, you perform this search using the Infoseek search engine.

To Refine Your Search

1 **Click the Search button in the Netscape toolbar.**

2 **Scroll down until you see the Infoseek search engine; then click that link. You may see a link to Infoseek at the top of the page. For the purposes of this exercise, don't use that link; rather, scroll down the page.**

Infoseek maintains a large database of Web pages and delivers a very comprehensive list of results.

3 **Type the keywords endangered species raptor in the search text box, separating the words by spaces (see Figure 7.6).**

continues

To Refine Your Search (continued)

Figure 7.6
Using Infoseek to refine
your search.

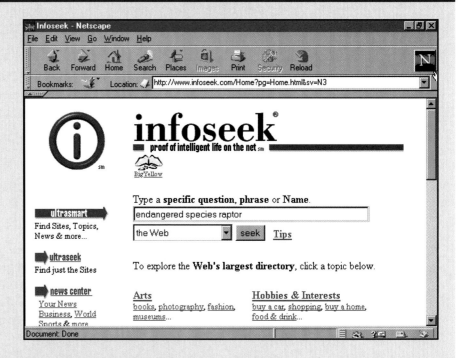

❹ **Click the seek button.**

Infoseek returns a large number of pages for your perusal—more
than you want. Next, you add another keyword to pull in information relating only to peregrine falcons.

❺ **Scroll to the bottom of the page.**

You see a blank text box.

❻ **Type the words peregrine falcon in the box.**

❼ **Click the radio button labeled** Search only these results **if it is
not already selected.**

This tells Infoseek to search *only* in the results of your original
search (see Figure 7.7).

Figure 7.7
Adding more keywords
to make your search
results more specific.

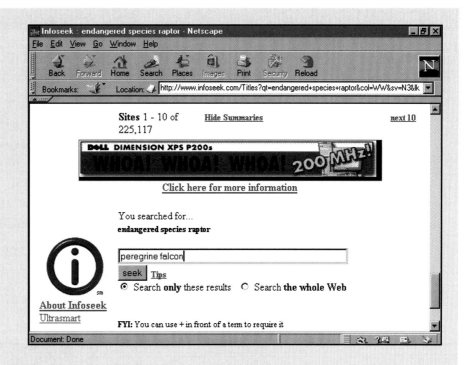

❽ Click the seek button.

Infoseek presents a variety of links and gives you the option to add
more keywords if you want even more specific search results.

❾ Select one of the links shown.

You use this link in the next lesson, where you learn to save and
print your findings.

Infoseek is also available at the following address:

http://www.infoseek.com

Lesson 4: Saving, Printing, or E-Mailing the Information You Found

If you have found some information that you consider pertinent to your
research, you are going to want to do something with the information so
that you can assess it at a later date. You have several options: saving, printing, or e-mailing the information you found.

To Save the Document

❶ **With the page that you want to save displayed on-screen, choose Save As from the File menu.**

The Save As dialog box is displayed, requesting a location where you want to save your document.

❷ **In the Save as type drop-down list box, select Plain Text if you want to be able to view your document through your word processing program (see Figure 7.8).**

Only the text will be saved; you won't be able to view any graphics. If you want to view the document through Netscape, select HTML Files.

Figure 7.8
Saving your document for future reference.

❸ **In the Save in drop-down list box, navigate to where you want to save your document; then click Save.**

Your document is now saved.

 Selecting Plain Text as your Save as **t**ype option will allow you to view the contents of the page later in any word processing program. Leave the **t**ype option as Source if you wish to view the page later using Netscape; however, the images will not show up on this version of the page.

To Print the Document

❶ With the page that you want to print displayed on-screen, choose Print from the File menu.

Alternately, you can click the Print button on the Netscape toolbar.

An option box is displayed asking you to confirm your print settings.

❷ Click OK or Print.

The name of the button will vary depending on your printer. Your document is then sent to the printer.

In the next exercise, you e-mail the document to yourself.

To E-Mail the Document to Yourself

❶ With the page that you want to mail displayed on-screen, choose Send Page from the File menu.

This command accesses Netscape Mail.

If you have problems...

In order for this option to work properly, make sure that you have your mail preferences set correctly. You can find your **M**ail and News Preferences by selecting Pr**e**ferences from the **E**dit menu. This step was described in Project 6.

❷ Fill in your e-mail address (see Figure 7.9).

Figure 7.9
Sending the information to yourself.

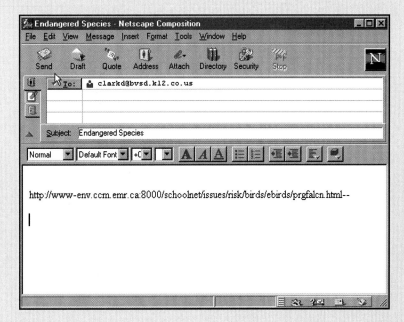

continues

To E-Mail the Document to Yourself (continued)

❸ **Click the Send button.**

The next time you check your e-mail, your message will be waiting for you.

❹ **Click the Back button to find another page that interests you.**

You are now ready to set a bookmark.

Lesson 5: Setting a Bookmark

Netscape enables you to set bookmarks for sites that you want to return to later. In this lesson, you set a bookmark to one of the links you found in the preceding lesson.

It is not always possible to set a bookmark at a page of search results. This page has dynamic information that was created specifically for you. However, a few search engines do allow you to set such a bookmark. Alta Vista, Lycos, and Infoseek are three that provide this service.

To Set a Bookmark

❶ **With the page that you want a bookmark set for displayed on-screen, choose Window, Bookmarks, and then Add Bookmark.**

The bookmark is now set (see Figure 7.10).

Figure 7.10
Setting a bookmark is a good way to ensure that you'll be able to find favorite pages when you need them.

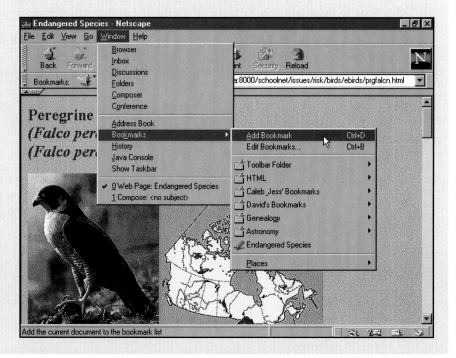

2 **To access your bookmark, choose the appropriate bookmark from the Bookmarks menu.**

Netscape automatically connects with that site. Note, however, that Web addresses can and will change frequently. If a Web site changes its address, your bookmark will no longer work.

If you have completed your session on the computer, exit Netscape and check with your instructor for further instructions. Otherwise, continue with "Checking Your Skills" at the end of this project.

Alta Vista can be found at the following address:

http://www.altavista.digital.com

Lycos can be found at this address:

http://www.lycos.com

Both of these search engines can also be accessed with the Search button on the Netscape toolbar.

Checking Your Skills

True/False

For each of the following, check *T* or *F* to indicate whether the statement is true or false.

__T __F **1.** The only way to access the search engines is to click the Search button in the Netscape toolbar.

__T __F **2.** All search engines enable you to refine your search results.

__T __F **3.** Search engines search only Web sites and not other Internet tools such as USENET.

__T __F **4.** You can set a bookmark for your search results page in all the search engines.

__T __F **5.** When saving a Web page document, select Plain Text as the Save as **t**ype option in the Save As dialog box if you want to view the document with your word processing program.

Multiple Choice

Circle the letter of the correct answer for each of the following.

1. Which of the following is *not* a Web search engine?

    a. Alta Vista

    b. Veronica

    c. Lycos

    d. all of these are Web search engines

2. If, at a later time, you want to access the information you've found in a document on the Web, which of the following methods can you use?

    a. Save the document as a text or HTML file.

    b. Mail the document to yourself.

    c. Set a bookmark to the document.

    d. all of the above

3. Which of the following search engines enables you to set a bookmark for your search results?

    a. Alta Vista

    b. Yahoo!

    c. Open Text

    d. none of the above—it is not possible to set a bookmark for search results pages

4. To define operators between your keywords using the Open Text search engine, you can do which of the following?

    a. Use the drop-down menus next to the words.

    b. Type the words *and* or *or* in the keyword text box.

    c. You cannot use operators in the Open Text search engine.

    d. a or b

5. You can access a wide variety of search engines by clicking which button in Netscape?

    a. Directory

    b. Search

    c. Net Search

    d. Yahoo!

Completion

In the blank provided, write the correct answer for each of the following statements.

1. Search engines return their results in the form of _____ to make it easier for the user to connect with the sites.

2. If your search results are too broad, some search engines give you the option of _____ your search results.

3. When typing keywords in a search text box, you must separate the words by a(n) _____.

4. Web pages are not the only places where search engines can look for information; they can search _____ as well.

5. You can access a search engine by clicking the appropriate button in the Netscape toolbar, or you can _____.

Applying Your Skills

Learning the ins and outs of the search engines available on the Internet will save you hours and hours as you search for information. Spend some time getting to know the search engines by completing the "On Your Own" and "Brief Cases" exercises; you won't regret it.

On Your Own

Comparing Search Engines

Each search engine has its own personality and will bring back different links for you to examine. In this exercise, you compare four different search engines.

To Compare Search Engines

1. Choose a topic of personal interest and define a keyword that you will use to search the Net.

2. Select four search engines and, one at a time, make a connection. You can access these engines by connecting directly to the URL or by clicking the Search button.

3. Compare your results. How many links did each search engine find? Did one engine seem to bring back more pertinent information on your topic?

4. Compare the results with those of other people in your class or around you. Is it possible to agree on which search engine is the best for everybody?

Performing this kind of exercise can help you decide which search engine to use first when you are starting to research a topic.

Brief Cases

Setting Customized Bookmarks for your Customers

It is almost a scary thought to use just the word *music* as your keyword in any search engine! Doing so is bound to bring back thousands and thousands of links, and sorting through them could take many hours. A service that you can provide to customers who come to your store is a set of preestablished bookmarks that customers can take home on disk. To provide this service, you need to know that your bookmark file is called bookmark.html and resides as a text file on your hard drive. This text file can be transferred to disk and shared with others.

To Create a Customized Bookmark File

1. Start Netscape.

2. Use your favorite search engine to research some good music sites. Ten sites should be enough for this exercise.

3. Set a bookmark for each site as you find it.

4. Exit Netscape and look in the Netscape folder on your hard drive for a file called bookmark.htm or bookmark.html.

If you can't find the file, use the find-file utility provided by your operating system to perform a search on your hard drive.

5. Transfer that file to a floppy disk by dragging the file icon to the floppy disk icon.

This bookmark file can now be duplicated and distributed. The file is a text file, and it can be manipulated to include more information. The file will contain a lot of funny characters that you may not recognize if you open it in a text editor, however. Project 8 explains what those characters mean and how you can enhance this file for distribution.

Project

8

Creating a Home Page

Objectives

In this project you learn how to:

- Create a Basic Home Page
- Add a List of Hyperlinks to Your Home Page
- Add a Graphic to Your Home Page
- Create a Table

Why Would I Do This?

Publishing on the World Wide Web is available to anyone who has access to a WWW server. This server may be on a UNIX machine where you have a dial-up account, or the server may be on a Mac or PC on your desktop. Having a home page on the Internet enables you to publish on the Web. You can share your ideas, advertise a product, make your resume available for prospective employers, and do much more.

Lesson 1: Creating a Basic Home Page

HTML (HyperText Markup Language)
A formatting language used in creating World Wide Web pages.

Most Web pages reside on UNIX servers on the Internet, although you can set up a page on a Macintosh or on a PC running Windows. In this lesson, you create a basic home page on a UNIX server. You use *HTML (HyperText Markup Language)* to design your home page.

To Create a Basic Home Page

1 Access your UNIX prompt.

You access the prompt through a Telnet utility or a dial-up connection.

2 At the UNIX prompt, type mkdir public_html and press ⏎Enter.

This command creates a directory in your UNIX account where you will store your home page.

3 Type chmod +x public_html and press ⏎Enter.

If you have problems...

While public_html works on most systems, some require that the html directory be named www. Check with your instructor to find the correct html directory name for your particular system.

UNIX enables its users to create permissions for certain files. This command turns on a permission, which, in effect, gives the world permission to see your home page. Without this step, your page would be inaccessible to the rest of the world.

4 Type cd public_html and press ⏎Enter.

This command moves you into your public_html directory, where you are ready to start designing.

You can use any text editor to make your home page. Pico is used in this example. If you have another editor, such as vi or joe, it will work just as well. Another option is to create your home page with your favorite word processing program and then cut and paste the page into a UNIX document.

⑤ Type pico home.html and press ⏎Enter.

After you press ⏎Enter, a new document entitled home.html opens. Your screen should now look like the one in Figure 8.1.

Figure 8.1
You are now ready to start designing your page.

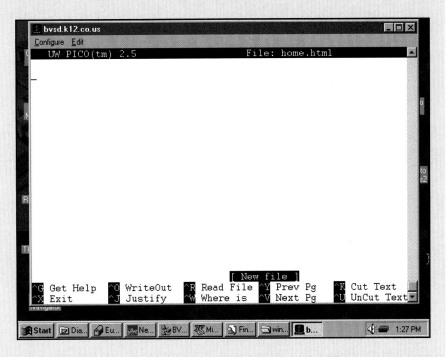

You are now ready to start designing the page itself. While working on a page, you will probably want to have two windows open at once, at least in the beginning. The window at the top, where the designing happens, is a window opened to pico. The window on the bottom will show how your page appears through Netscape. Once your page gets too big to view with split windows, you'll need to keep one window in the background. You can then move back and forth between the windows by using Alt+Tab⇆ or by clicking on a part of the window you want active.

Nearly every html command has this form:

    <tag>text</tag>

Tag
A piece of HTML code; tags usually occur in pairs that define how a World Wide Web browser will display the information between the tags.

One of the most forgotten elements is the slash (/) in the second tag. If your page doesn't work, look there first. The information within the angle brackets (< >) is formatting information that Netscape or other Web browsers will read and interpret.

Any text that is not surrounded by a pair of *tags* will appear as straight text on your page, as viewed through Netscape or other browser.

continues

❻ With the top window open to the PICO editor, type the following:

```
<html>

<head>

<title>My Home Page</title>

</head>

<body>

</body>

</html>
```

Notice that for every tag there is a corresponding tag that includes a / in it, such as <html> and </html>.

❼ Save your work by pressing Ctrl+X **(if you are using pico).**

❽ At your UNIX prompt type chmod a+r home.html.

As before in step 3, we gave others permissions to enter our public_html directory, now we use the chmod command to give them permission to see our html page.

❾ Type pico home.html and press ↵Enter**.**

This puts you back in the PICO editor so you can make further changes to your page.

❿ Open Netscape.

Do not quit your Telnet session; leave that open as well.

⓫ Resize your windows so that the two open programs, Telnet and Netscape, share the desktop.

⓬ In the Netscape location box, type the URL for your home page and then press ↵Enter**.**

Generally, a URL to a personal home page will have this format:

http://host.address/~username/pagename.html

In most of the examples used in this book, the host address is stripe.colorado.edu. (This is usually the last part of your e-mail address—after the @.)

The username is dclark. Don't forget the ~ (tilde) before it.

The pagename used is home.html. You can call your page anything you like as long as the .html extension is present.

The full URL for this page, then, is the following:

http://stripe.colorado.edu/~dclark/home.html

After you save the text, the page should look similar to the one in Figure 8.2. As noted, the page is being designed in the top window. How it looks through Netscape is shown in the bottom window. Notice that the words My Home Page appear in the window title.

Figure 8.2
Designing your home page.

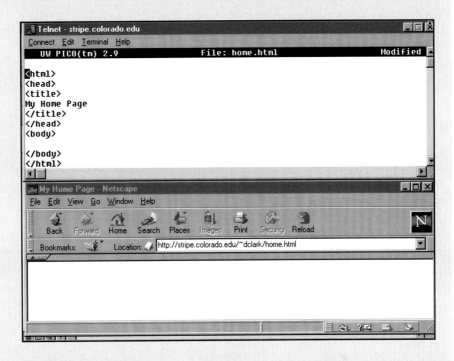

You need to save any changes in your text editor before you can see them in Netscape. You also need to reload the page in Netscape. To save your changes, press Ctrl+O while in pico, then press ↵Enter. To reload the page, click the Reload button on the Netscape toolbar.

⓭ Click Reload.

You are now ready to fill in the page. Notice that the words My Home Page do not appear on the page itself. Text that is included between the <title> and </title> tags appears only in the title bar of the window itself. The real meat of your page will be created between the <body></body> tags.

⓮ Between the <body> and </body> tags, type the following:

<h1>My Home Page</h1>

⓯ Press Ctrl+O followed by ↵Enter.

This command saves your work.

You can assign to a piece of text one of six levels of header emphasis. <h1> is the largest, and <h6> is the smallest. Because this header goes at the top of the page, choose the largest header to grab the attention of the reader (see Figure 8.3).

continues

To Create a Basic Home Page (continued)

Figure 8.3
An <h1> header.

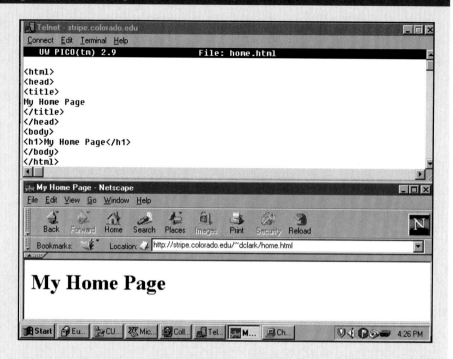

16 **Type <hr> and save your work by pressing Ctrl+O followed by ↵Enter.**

This code places a horizontal line below the header.

17 **Below the <hr> tag, write some text about yourself and then save your work when you are finished.**

You do not need to encompass this text between any tags other than the ones that are already there.

18 **Bring the Netscape window to the front and maximize it.**

19 **To view your page in Netscape, click the Reload button.**

At this point, your page will be getting too large to view both the source code and the page as it is being designed. Therefore, you will need to use Alt+Tab⇆ to move between the two windows.

When you view your page through Netscape or another browser, the page should appear similar to Figure 8.4.

You should still have two programs open, one for the Telnet session where you are designing your page, and one for Netscape where you can view your creation as you work on it. Leave both of these programs open for use in the next lesson.

Figure 8.4
A basic Web page.

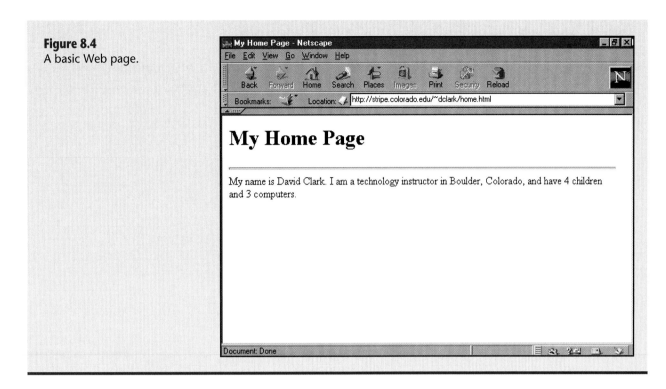

Here are a few more tags that you may want to use to format your text:

<b> </b>	Makes the text bold.
<i> </i>	Makes the text italic.
<center> </center>	Centers a block of text or a graphic.
 	Places a line break at the end of the line. Notice that this tag can exist by itself and does not require a </br> to complement it.
<p>	Places a paragraph break at the end of the line. This tag is similar to except that <p> not only places a carriage return but also adds a blank line.

Lesson 2: Adding a List of Hyperlinks to Your Home Page

Most World Wide Web pages contain hyperlinks to other sites on the Web. These are the clickable links that connect your page with the rest of the world. In this lesson, you put these links in a bulleted list.

To Add a List of Hyperlinks to Your Home Page

❶ Bring the design screen to the front and type <ul> below the text you wrote in Lesson 1.

This is the opening HTML tag that tells your Web browser to read the text that follows the tag as a bulleted, unnumbered list. At the end of the list, you include the </ul> tag to close the command.

❷ Type the following exactly as shown:

>   **<li><a href="http://www.yahoo.com">Yahoo</a>**
>
>   **<li><a href="http://www.mcp.com">Macmillan Home Page</a>**
>
>   **</ul>**

The first two lines create links to other sites.

The <li> indicates that these are elements of the list. The <a href="..." is the address to which your Web browser connects.

The words between the > < (Yahoo! and Macmillan Home Page) will appear on-screen as clickable links. Figure 8.5 shows how your design screen should look at this point.

Figure 8.5
Designing a Web page with clickable links.

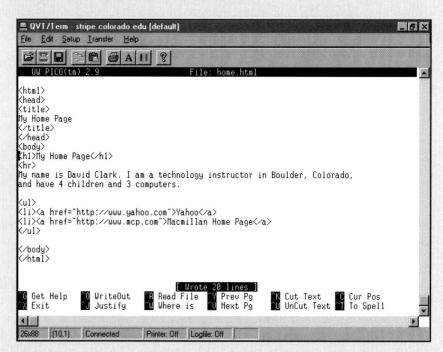

❸ Save your work in pico by pressing Ctrl+X **followed by** ↵Enter.

❹ Bring the Netscape window to the front and click the Reload button.

This saves your work and displays it through Netscape. The page should appear as in Figure 8.6.

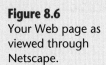

Figure 8.6
Your Web page as viewed through Netscape.

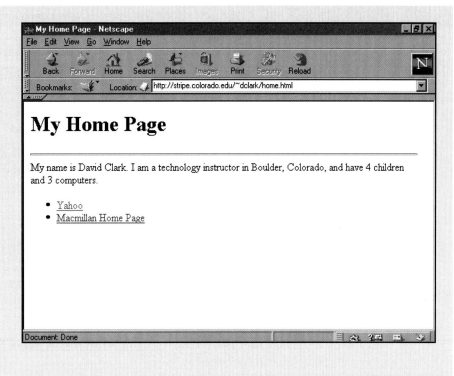

Leave Netscape and Telnet open. In the next lesson, you learn how to place a graphic on your page.

You can include other kinds of lists in your HTML document. Here are the tags:

<ol> </ol>	Creates an ordered list. Each list item will be preceded by a number corresponding to its place in the list.
<dl> </dl>	Creates a definition list. This type of list is usually used for a glossary or a similar list of terms with associated descriptions. The tag <dt> is placed before the term and <dd> before the description.

Lesson 3: Adding a Graphic to Your Home Page

You can easily include graphics on your home page if you like. The image must meet the following conditions:

➤ It should preferably be saved in the .gif or .jpeg/.jpg format.

➤ The HTML source code <img src ="graphic.gif"> must be included in your HTML document; the name of the graphic replaces graphic.gif.

➤ You must place the graphic into your public_html directory. This can be a little tricky. You can use an FTP utility such as Fetch or Ws_FTP to upload an original or scanned graphic. You can also transfer a graphic from an existing graphics archive. Several such archives are available.

In this lesson, you transfer an "under construction" graphic and place it on your home page.

To Add a Graphic to Your Home Page

❶ Quit pico by pressing Ctrl+X **followed by** ↵Enter.

❷ At your UNIX prompt, type the following:

lynx http://www.iconbazaar.com

This connects you with a graphics archive.

Make sure that you are in your public_html directory when you type this command. Lynx is the text-based WWW browser introduced in Project 6. You will use Lynx to access a graphics archive and transfer a file into your public_html directory.

Note: Because you are using Lynx, you will not be able to view the graphics in the archive. If you want to see the graphics in this archive, connect to the preceding URL using Netscape. However, you do not want to use Netscape to transfer the graphic because Netscape will transfer the file to your local hard drive, not to your UNIX public_html directory.

❸ Use your arrow keys to highlight Signs and Logos **and then press** ↵Enter.

You may need to scroll down the page to find this entry. Press Spacebar in Lynx to move down a page. You have now moved into a graphics archive where you will be able to transfer a graphic into your own directory.

❹ Use ↓ **to highlight the graphic entitled uconstr1.gif; then press** ↵Enter.

Lynx displays the following message, as shown in Figure 8.7:

```
This file cannot be displayed on this terminal:  D)ownload, or
C)ancel
```

Figure 8.7
Transferring a file using Lynx.

5 **Press Ⓓ to download the file.**

Lynx downloads the file and presents the following options:

```
Save to disk

Use Kermit to download to the local terminal

Use Zmodem to download to the local terminal
```

`Save to disk` will be highlighted.

6 **Press ⏎Enter twice.**

The file transfer is now complete. Because you were in your public_html directory when you connected with this graphics archive, the file is transferred into that directory.

While you are connected to this graphics site, you can take a look around to see what other graphics you might want to transfer. If you want to view the graphics first before you transfer them, open the URL using Netscape.

7 **Press Ⓠ. You quit Lynx and return to your UNIX prompt.**

8 **Type pico home.html.**

This opens your home.html document.

9 **Insert the tag <img src = "uconstr1.gif">.**

This includes the graphic in your home page, as shown in Figure 8.8. You place this tag at the top of your page, just below the <body> tag. You can also include the following words:

This Page Is Under Construction

Figure 8.8
Using the graphic tag in your home page.

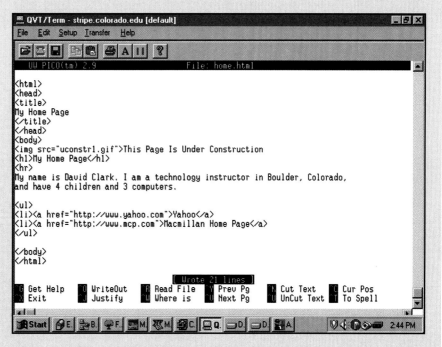

continues

To Add a Graphic to Your Home Page (continued)

⑩ **Save your work in pico and bring the Netscape window to the front.**

⑪ **View your page through Netscape by clicking the Reload button.**

Your graphic should now appear as in Figure 8.9.

Figure 8.9
Placing a graphic on your Web page.

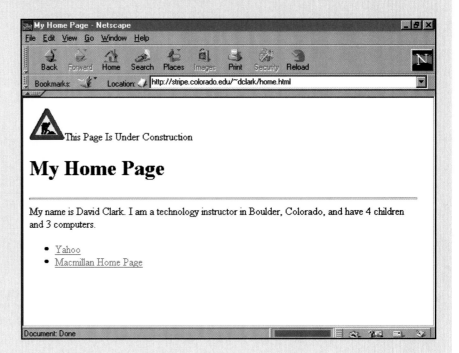

In the next lesson, you learn how to create a table to place on your page.

If you want to change the size of the graphic on your page, you can use the height and width commands. For example, you can type the following:

<img src="uconstr1.gif" height=200 width=200>

Experiment with different sizes until you get the effect you are looking for.

Lesson 4: Creating a Table

A common formatting tool used by many Web designers is a table. You can use tables to organize your information, create a calendar, or present your information in many ways. In this lesson, you create a table to display the different multimedia extensions found on the Internet and to indicate what they mean.

To Create a Table

❶ Bring the design screen to the front.

❷ Position your cursor below your list and links and press ⏎Enter to move down a line.

❸ Type <table border> and then press ⏎Enter to move to the next line.

You can leave out the word *border* if you want. Including it places a border around your table.

❹ Type the following command and press ⏎Enter:

<tr><th>Extension</th><th>Multimedia Type</th></tr>

This command creates a table with two columns. The <th> </th> tags inform your browser that these are table headers. The <tr> </tr> tags tell the browser that this information will be contained on a single row.

❺ Type the following command and press ⏎Enter:

<tr><td>.mpg</td><td>Video</td></tr>

This positions .mpg below the Extensions heading and positions Video below the Multimedia Type heading. <td> </td> defines that these are table elements, and <tr> </tr> again tells the browser that this is a single row in the table.

❻ Type the following and press ⏎Enter:

<tr><td>.wav</td><td>Sound</td></tr>

❼ Type the following and press ⏎Enter:

<tr><td>.gif</td><td>Graphic</td></tr>

❽ Type </table> to close the <table> tag that you created in step 1.

Your design screen should now look like Figure 8.10.

❾ To save your work, press Ctrl+O and press ⏎Enter.

❿ Bring the Netscape window to the front and click the Reload button.

Your table should now appear as in Figure 8.11.

continues

To Create a Table (continued)

Figure 8.10
HTML code for creating
a table.

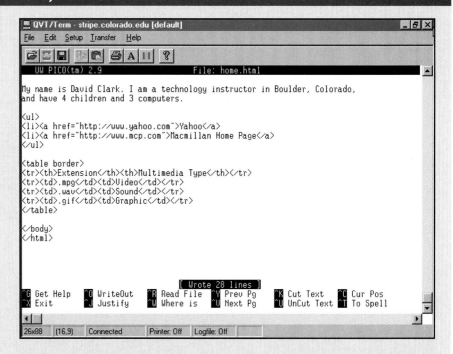

Figure 8.11
Your table viewed
through Netscape.

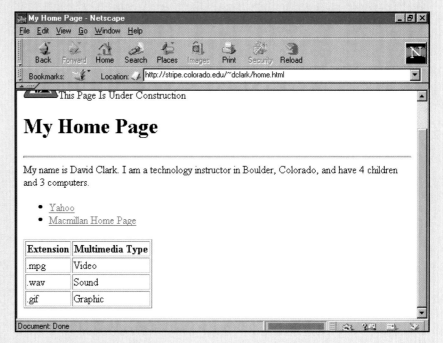

If you have completed your session on the computer, quit your text editor and log out of your Telnet session. Then exit Netscape and check with your instructor for further instructions. Otherwise, continue with the "Checking Your Skills" section at the end of this project.

Using HTML Editors

Many HTML editors are available to make the job of creating an HTML document simpler. HotDog, FrontPage, Pagemill, Internet Assistant for Word, and WebWeaver are a few of the names you might encounter. When you use an HTML editor, you create and edit the page on your local hard drive. HTML editors have point-and-click interfaces. If, for example, you want a section in bold, you just highlight the text and select the Bold option from the menu or toolbar, as shown in Figure 8.12. The editor then fills in the appropriate tags for you.

You can do many tasks, such as creating tables or formatting text, in this way. Once you have completed your design, you need to use an FTP utility such as Fetch or Ws_FTP to upload your home page into your public_html directory.

Another exciting Web design option is *WYSIWYG* ("What You See Is What You Get") HTML editors. This new generation of Web page design software hides the tags from your view. If you want bold, you see bold on the screen instead of the <b> </b> tags surrounding your text. One such editor is Netscape Gold. It enables you to design your page in a Netscape window. You can retrieve this editor from ftp://ftp.netscape.com.

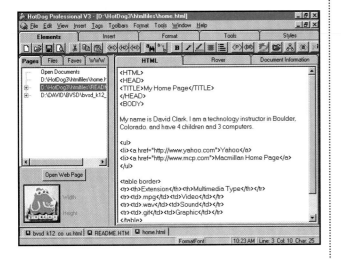

Figure 8.12
Using an HTML editor.

By using these tags, you can create a wide variety of Web pages with different looks. This project only scratches the surface, however. If you are interested in finding out more about how to create Web pages, you can take a look at the following:

```
http://www.yahoo.com/Computers_and_Internet/Software/Data_Formats/HTML/
Guides_and_Tutorials/
```

Here you will find a variety of links that can take you to the next level of Web page designing.

Another good strategy is to view what other people have done. If you see a page that you particularly like, you can view the source with Netscape. To do this, select Source from the **V**iew menu, and you will then see the HTML coding required to create that particular page.

Checking Your Skills

True/False

For each of the following statements, check *T* or *F* to indicate whether the statement is true or false.

__T __F **1.** All HTML tags have two components, one at the beginning of a piece of text and the other at the end.

__T __F **2.** The second tag in a pair of tags will always include a /.

__T __F **3.** HTML stands for HyperText Markup Language.

__T _F **4.** All Web pages exist on UNIX servers.

__T __F **5.** A table must always include a border.

Multiple Choice

Circle the letter of the correct answer for each of the following.

1. Which set of tags would you use to highlight a piece of text in bold?

    a. <b> </b>

    b.

    c. <i> </i>

    d. <b> <b>

2. The <br> tag _____.

    a. places an empty space between two lines

    b. creates a line break without an empty space

    c. puts a horizontal line across the screen

    d. There is no such thing as a <br> tag.

3. To view a newly edited page in Netscape, you must _____.

    a. save your work on the design screen

    b. reload Netscape or start it up

    c. quit the application you are using to design the page

    d. a and b

4. In the URL http://your.domain/~your.login/home.html, home.html represents _____.

    a. the host you are connecting with

    b. the name of the file of your home page

    c. part of the directory path to your home page

    d. none of the above

5. The command to save your work in pico is _____.

    a. Ctrl+C

    b. Ctrl+O

    c. Ctrl+S

    d. Ctrl+Q

Completion

In the blank provided, write the correct answer for each of the following statements.

1. Selecting **So**urce from the **V**iew menu in Netscape enables you to _____.

2. Using Netscape to download a graphic will transfer that graphic to _____.

3. You can use any _____ to create your home page.

4. In the HTML code <a href="http://www.yahoo.com">Yahoo</a>, the word *Yahoo* will _____.

5. The <table border> tag differs from the <table> tag in that _____.

Applying Your Skills

The Web is where all the creative stuff on the Internet happens. Take a few minutes to practice the skills you have learned in this project by completing the "On Your Own" and "Brief Cases" exercises.

On Your Own

Creating an Online Resume

Won't a prospective employer be impressed when you tell that person that he or she can view your resume on the Web? Create a Web page with information about yourself, with perhaps a picture. (To do this, you can either scan a photo by using a scanner, or take a picture with a digital camera if you have one available to you.)

To Design Your Resume

1. Access your UNIX prompt and move into your public_html directory.

2. Use pico to create a document called resume.html.

3. Create a table at the top of the page to highlight the major components of your resume, such as Education and Work Experience.

4. Use the tag **<a href="#education">Education</a>** within the table to make the word *Education* a clickable link.

This creates a clickable link within the table that will reference your Education section in the same document. You can do the same with other resume sections, such as Work Experience and Personal Information.

5. At the beginning of your Education section, place the reference **<a name="education"></a>**.

This anchors the reference so that the clickable link created in step 4 knows where to go.

Brief Cases

Announcing Your Presence on the Web

The largest growing segment of the World Wide Web is the commercial sector. Business owners all over the world are putting up Web pages to attract new customers and provide better support to their existing clientele. However, your first goal is to let the world know that you have a presence on the Web. One of the first steps in establishing your presence is to register yourself with the existing search engines. Many of the search engines let you do this right from their home pages; look for a link such as Add URL.

You can also access a FAQ on the Net that will give you tips on how and where to announce your page.

To Obtain Information on Announcing Your Web Page

1. Open Netscape.

2. In the Location box that appears, type the following:

http://ep.com/faq/webannounce.html

Spend some time reading this document. When you are ready, jump in and start letting the world know that you exist on the Web.

Appendix

Working with UNIX

Objectives

In this appendix you learn how to:

- Access the UNIX Prompt
- Navigate Your Home Directory
- Create and View a Text Document
- Move, Rename, and Copy Files
- Find Out Who Else is Online
- Initiate a Talk Session with Another User
- Respond to a Talk Session
- Exit from a UNIX Session

What Is UNIX?

UNIX is the operating system of choice on the Internet. Probably more than half of the computers that connect to the Internet run some form of an operating system called UNIX. UNIX is a command-based operating system, which was not created with you or me in mind. It was created to be functional, not friendly. It survived and thrived in an environment filled with computer scientists, physicists, and engineers—people who weren't thinking about how to create a helpful system that ordinary people could use.

As a dial-in user, you connect with a computer that is more than likely running UNIX. If you are in a lab with a dedicated connection, you need to use a Telnet utility, such as QVTNet or Telnet for Windows, or NCSA Telnet for Macintosh, to get to the UNIX prompt.

The Internet is thought of as a way to connect to the world. Most people don't realize that when they connect through a UNIX prompt, they are entering a new level of computing power. For the dial-up user, UNIX is a command line interpreter's nightmare (or dream, depending on your point of view).

It isn't necessary to become a UNIX guru to get on the Internet. New interfaces are being developed that hide the shortcomings of UNIX. Working from a direct connection or with a SLIP connection will help you avoid having to deal with UNIX.

Lesson 1: Accessing the UNIX Prompt

If you are connecting through a dial-up connection (the examples in this appendix use a dial-up connection), the first thing you will probably see, after entering your login name and password, is the UNIX prompt. If your instructor or system administrator has set up your computer with a menu from which to choose, you may see an option to get to the prompt. Prompts differ from computer to computer. The following are some examples of different prompts:

```
$

csh>

sparc%
```

At the prompt, you can enter commands to tell the computer what to do. Figure A.1 shows an example of a typical UNIX prompt.

Figure A.1
A typical UNIX prompt.

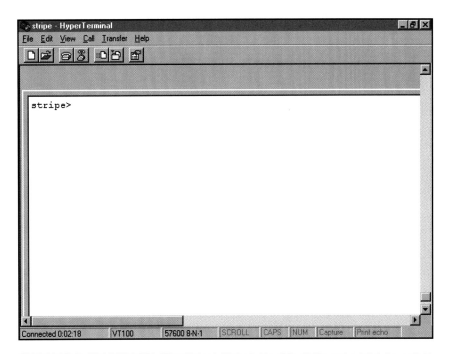

Lesson 2: Navigating Your Home Directory

When you first log on, you are in the home directory, which is also the current or working directory (that is, the one you are in at the moment). In this lesson, you explore what is in your home directory.

1. At the UNIX prompt, type **ls -F** and press ⏎Enter.

This lets you view the contents of your home directory. Alternatively, you may be able to type **dir** at the UNIX prompt to find this information. Your screen will look similar to Figure A.2—similar because each system is set up a bit differently.

Figure A.2
The contents of a home directory.

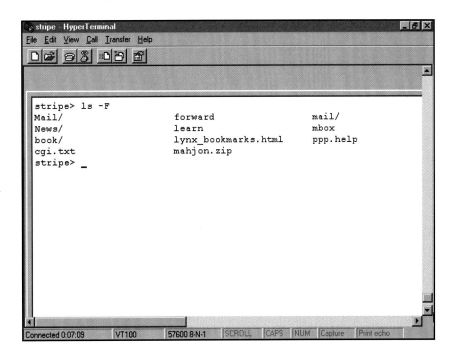

What you are looking at are the directories and files in your home directory. Notice that some of these end with a /, which indicates that they are directories. If you are entering your home directory for the first time, you won't have many directories from which to choose.

2. Type **mkdir test** at the UNIX prompt and press ⏎Enter.

This creates a new directory called *test* within your home directory.

3. Type **ls -F** again and press ⏎Enter.

This lets you view the contents of the directory. You should now see your directory listed, as shown in Figure A.3.

Figure A.3
Your first directory.

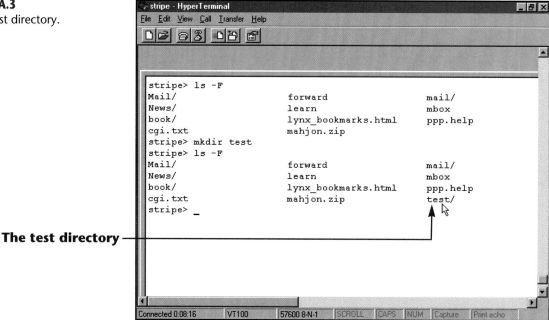

The test directory

4. Type **cd test** and press ⏎Enter.

This moves you into that directory, but nothing is in the directory at this time.

Lesson 3: Creating and Viewing a Text Document

Next, you create a text document to place inside the directory you just created.

1. Type **pico test.file** at the UNIX prompt and press ⏎Enter.

UNIX is, in nearly every instance, case-sensitive. The use of lowercase for commands is generally preferred, so be sure to type all the UNIX commands given in this appendix exactly as you see them.

You should now be in the pico text editor. Notice that this is the same editor used for sending e-mail in Pine.

Pico is a popular text editor found on many UNIX systems. If pico doesn't work for you, ask your instructor or system administrator which editors are on your system.

2. Type a message.

Figure A.4 shows an example of a message.

Figure A.4

Creating a document in pico.

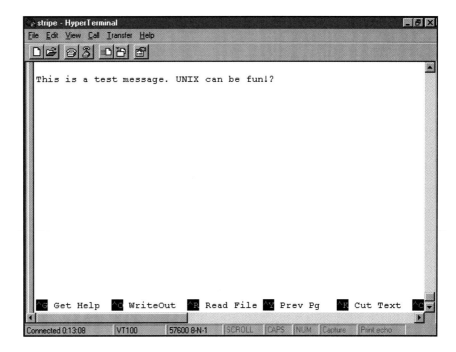

3. Exit pico by pressing Ctrl+X.

You then see the prompt Save modified buffer (ANSWERING "No" WILL DESTROY CHANGES) ?.

4. Press Y or simply press ↵Enter.

Pico then displays the prompt File Name to write : test.file.

5. Press Y or ↵Enter.

You are returned to the UNIX prompt.

6. Type **ls -F** once again and press ↵Enter.

This time you should see your file listed, as shown in Figure A.5.

7. Type **more test.file** at the UNIX prompt and press ↵Enter.

The *more* command is used to view the contents of a text file a page at a time. This file has only a single page, of course, but if it were longer, you could advance to the next page by pressing the Spacebar.

8. Type **cd ..** and press ↵Enter.

This is the command to move up a directory. The command takes you out of the directory created for this lesson and back to your top-level home directory.

Figure A.5
test.file is the document you created using pico.

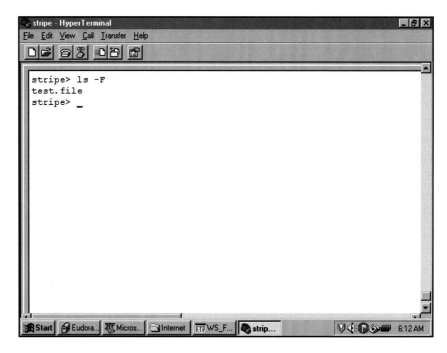

```
stripe> ls -F
test.file
stripe> _
```

Table A.1 lists the commands you just used to create and move in and out of a directory.

Table A.1 UNIX Commands	
Command	To
ls -F	List what is in the directory
cd <directory name>	Change directories
more <file name>	Print a file to the screen
cd ..	Move up a directory
mkdir <directory name>	Create a directory

Many more files are available in your home directory than you can actually see when you use the ls command. Many of these files are used to set your user preferences. You can view the entire contents of your home directory by typing the **ls -a** command.

Some of the files you may find include the following:

.login	Read by the computer each time you log in. The environmental setting, such as your prompt, and the terminal type are set here.
.cshrc/.kshrc	Another initialization file called up when entering the UNIX shell account.
.Pinerc	Settings for the Pine mailing program.
.newsrc	A list of newsgroups by your server.
.lynxrc	Settings for the World Wide Web browser Lynx.

You can view the contents of any of these by using the more command, as in the following example:

```
stripe>more .login
```

This command shows you the contents of your .login.

Lesson 4: Moving, Renaming, and Copying Files

In this lesson, you manipulate some of the files in the directory you just created.

1. At the UNIX prompt, type **cd test** and press ⏎Enter.

This moves you to your test directory. You will use test.file, the file you created in the preceding lesson, to learn about altering files.

2. Type **ls -F** to list the files in that directory.

You should see the file test.file listed.

3. Type **mv test.file test** at the UNIX prompt and press ⏎Enter .

This renames the file test.file as test. The *mv* command is versatile in that it is used for renaming and moving files. UNIX first looks for a destination. For example, if a directory called test exists, test would be moved inside that directory. However, because no such directory exists, UNIX assumes that you want to rename the file.

4. Type **ls -F** and press ⏎Enter.

This lists the files in the test directory (see Figure A.6). You should now see a file named test.

Figure A.6
Using the mv command to rename your files.

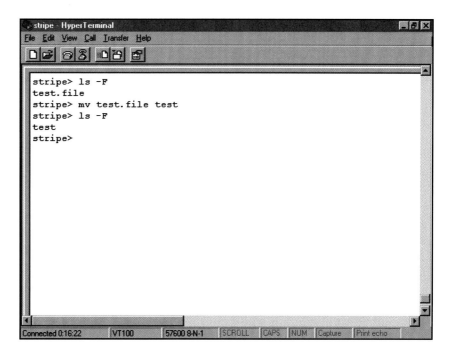
```
stripe> ls -F
test.file
stripe> mv test.file test
stripe> ls -F
test
stripe>
```

5. Type **cp test test2** and press ⏎Enter (see Figure A.7).

The *cp* command is used to copy a file while leaving the original intact.

6. Type **ls -F** at the prompt and press ⏎Enter.

You now have two files in your directory, one called test and the other test2. UNIX assumes that you want to create the file in the same directory as the original. You can place the file anywhere you like by defining the path to the new directory.

Figure A.7
Copying your files.

Table A.2 lists the commands you just used to rename and copy your file.

Table A.2 More UNIX Commands	
Command	To
mv <filename> <new location>	Move a file. If the new location is a directory within your current directory, just typing the name of the directory is enough. If the directory exists elsewhere, you will have to include the path to that directory.
mv <filename> <new filename>	Change the name of the file. The same command is used to move and rename a file. If a location doesn't exist, UNIX assumes that you want to rename the file.
cp <filename> <location or new name>	Create a copy of a file in a new location or with a different file name.
pwd	Tell you which directory you are currently in. Stands for print working directory.

Lesson 5: Finding Out Who Else Is Online

At times, you may want to find out who else is online or find some information about other users. Here is how to do it.

1. Return to the UNIX prompt if you are not already there.

It doesn't matter which directory you are in when you issue the *finger* command.

2. Type **finger** and press ⏎Enter.

This enables you to find out who is online at the same time that you are on your host computer (see Figure A.8). The finger command can also be used to find people on your system. The command `finger <name>` lists everyone with the name you have typed who has an account on the same computer you are using.

Figure A.8
The results of issuing the finger command.

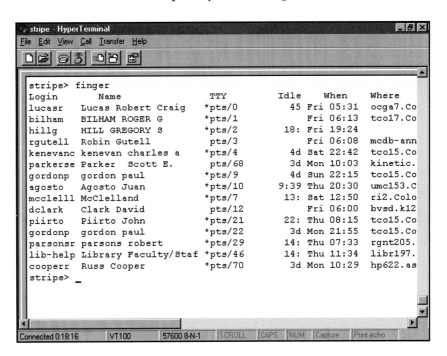

```
stripe> finger
Login      Name               TTY        Idle    When      Where
lucasr     Lucas Robert Craig *pts/0       45 Fri 05:31    ocga7.Co
bilham     BILHAM ROGER G     *pts/1          Fri 06:13    tco17.Co
hillg      HILL GREGORY S     *pts/2       18: Fri 19:24
rgutell    Robin Gutell       pts/3           Fri 06:08    mcdb-ann
kenevanc   kenevan charles a  *pts/4       4d Sat 22:42    tco15.Co
parkerse   Parker  Scott E.   pts/68       3d Mon 10:03    kinetic.
gordonp    gordon paul        *pts/9       4d Sun 22:15    tco15.Co
agosto     Agosto Juan        *pts/10    9:39 Thu 20:30    umc153.C
mcclelll   McClelland         *pts/7       13: Sat 12:50   ri2.Colo
dclark     Clark David        pts/12          Fri 06:00    bvsd.k12
piirto     Piirto John        *pts/21      22: Thu 08:15   tco15.Co
gordonp    gordon paul        *pts/22      3d Mon 21:55    tco15.Co
parsonsr   parsons robert     *pts/29      14: Thu 07:33   rgnt205.
lib-help   Library Faculty/Staf *pts/46    14: Thu 11:34   libr197.
cooperr    Russ Cooper        *pts/70      3d Mon 10:29    hp622.as
stripe> _
```

3. Type **finger <your first name>**.

For example, typing **finger david** at the UNIX prompt would bring up a list of all the Davids on your host computer (see Figure A.9). This also provides the login name and the last time each person logged in.

If you only know the first or last name of an individual, you can use the finger command to find that person's login name. For example, the command **finger dclark** would display the following information:

```
Login name: dclark                    In real life: Clark David

Directory:  /home/dclark                            Shell:
/usr/local/etc/CNSlogin

On since Dec 27 06:00:01 on pts/12 from bvsd.k12.co.us

New mail received Thu Dec 26 15:13:51 1996;

  unread since Thu Dec 26 06:24:30 1996

No Plan.
```

Figure A.9
A list of other Davids on
mcp.com.

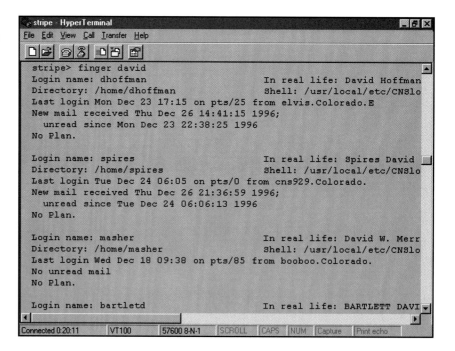

The *who* (or *w*) command also shows who is online at the same time as you. This command goes one step beyond the finger command in that it also shows you what the other users are doing online. For example, typing **w** displays the following results:

User	tty	from	login@	idle	JCPU	PCPU	what
mminerva	p0	cns956.Colorad	5:58pm		18	18	-csh
johnsd	p2	tco5.Colorado.	7:13am	12:27	1:42	1:42	kermit
mismith	p3	tco9.Colorado.	7:07pm		3	3	pine
sconvers	pa	tco5.Colorado.	7:32am	11:48			-
clarkd	q9	tco13.Colorado	7:09pm				w

The login name is on the left. The far right column tells which command was last issued to the computer. For example, mismith is currently using Pine, and johnsd is using kermit to download a file.

Lesson 6: Initiating a Talk Session with Another User

It is possible to talk interactively with another user on a UNIX system if you are both online at the same time.

1. Type **mesg y** and press ⏎Enter.

You have to give other users permission to talk with you. This setting may be the default. When you no longer want to receive talk requests from other users, type **mesg n** to turn off the permissions for that session. You can discover the default setting by typing **mesg** at the prompt and pressing ⏎Enter.

2. Type **w** and press ⏎Enter.

Look for a user who is not presently engaged in sending or receiving e-mail, a Lynx session, or an FTP session. Select a user whose far right column reads -csh, -tcsh, or -ksh, which indicates that the user is currently at the UNIX prompt. It is considered rude to request a talk session with someone who is occupied with a task.

3. Type **ytalk <username>**.

If this command doesn't work, use the word *talk* instead of *ytalk*. This lets you enter into an interactive chat with one or more user who is online. Your screen will split, and you can write and read simultaneously if you want. Spend some time writing and exploring.

4. Press Ctrl+C.

This exits you from the session.

Lesson 7: Responding to a Talk Session

If someone requests a talk session with you, a message similar to the following will appear on your screen:

```
Message from Talk_Daemon@bvsd.k12.co.us at 20:01

talk: connection requested by msmith@spot.Colorado.EDU

talk: respond with:  talk msmith@spot.Colorado.EDU
```

To respond, type **talk msmith@spot.Colorado.EDU** at the UNIX prompt. You should then be in an interactive chat session. Everything that you type on your screen will appear on the screen of the person you are connected with, and vice versa.

Lesson 8: Exiting from a UNIX Session

Quitting your UNIX session is very important. If you leave your session open and walk away from your computer, anyone can access your account. This means that someone else can send e-mail in your name or harass other users with talk requests that appear to be coming from you. Never forget to log out.

1. At the UNIX prompt, type **logout** and press `←Enter`.

   Your UNIX session is terminated. Alternatively, you can type **exit** or press `Ctrl`+`D` to end your session.

2. From the **F**ile menu, choose E**x**it.

   This closes your communications software, and you are done.

Table A.3 lists some other commands that you might find useful.

Table A.3 Miscellaneous Commands	
Command	To
passwd	Change your password
man -k <keyword>	Bring up a help file on a specific topic
learn	Help you learn UNIX (on most systems)
exit or logout	Exit your session

The commands covered in this appendix barely scratch the surface of what you can do with UNIX. If you would like to learn more, you can subscribe to several newsgroups, including comp.unix.questions, comp.unix.wizards, and comp.unix.misc.

For more information on UNIX, refer to *Inside UNIX*, Second Edition, by Chris Hare (Indianapolis, IN: New Riders, 1995) or *Using UNIX*, by Larry Schumer and Chris Negus (Indianapolis, IN: Que, 1995).

GLOSSARY

alias   A simple name that is substituted for a command name to make it easier to remember. A UNIX example is **alias oakland ftp oak.oakland.edu**. This creates an alias so that you just need to type **oakland** to make an FTP connection to oak.oakland.edu.

America Online   An online information service that provides e-mail, discussion groups, file downloading, and Internet access for a monthly fee.

Anonymous FTP   A system in which you, as a user of the Internet, can download files from certain sites without needing a login name and password. You use *anonymous* as your login name, and your e-mail address as your password.

Archie   An Internet utility for searching FTP sites around the world.

ASCII   Stands for American Standard Code for Information Interchange. A standard for computer-generated characters, such as numbers, letters, and symbols.

article   A posting in a UseNet newsgroup.

bandwidth   A measurement of the amount of data that can be transferred over the network at any given time. The greater the bandwidth, the more data that can move at once.

baud   The speed at which a modem can physically transfer data. The maximum baud rate for most modems and PCs is 33,600 baud. Contrast this to bps.

BBS   Stands for Bulletin Board System. A computer system, often local, where users can dial in with their modems to share information, play games, download files, and so on. These systems are often located in your neighbors' basements.

BFN   Stands for "Bye, For Now."

BinHex   A method by which Macintosh binary files (programs, graphics, and formatted text) are converted into ASCII text. This method enables the file to be transferred via e-mail. The file has to be "debinhexed" on the other end before it can be used.

bps   Stands for bits per second. A measurement of the number of bits that can be transferred per second over a line. Up to 9,600, baud and bps are the same. For bps rates higher than 9,600, the transfer is happening at 9,600 baud, but the data is being compressed so that the number of bits transferred per second increases.

BTW   Stands for "By The Way."

chat   To write interactively online with another user. When you chat with someone, your typed words appear on that person's screen (nearly) simultaneously with your own.

client   A piece of software used to access the Internet that acts on your behalf. Gopher is client software that retrieves information from the Internet for you. A client can also be a computer system that uses the resources of another computer on the network.

CompuServe   An online information service that offers e-mail, forums, file downloading, news, and more. CompuServe is known for being more business-oriented than other online services. CompuServe offers Internet e-mail and UseNet newsgroups and may be offering more Internet features in the near future.

compressed file   A file that is condensed to take up less disk space or to transfer faster. You must decompress the file with a decompression utility before you can use it.

cyberspace   When is a space not a space? When it's the "space" you enter when you log onto an online service or connect to the Internet. Cyberspace is the virtual arena where computer-mediated communication takes place.

dedicated connection A cable connection between your computer and the host computer. It's "on" all the time, even when you're not using it, and the line (cable) is "dedicated" for that use—it has no other purpose. Direct connections are very fast, making them ideal for graphical software use. Contrast this to dial-up terminal and dial-up direct connections.

dedicated line A high-speed telephone line that is permanently wired into the Internet. This line moves information directly from your computer to the rest of the Internet.

dial-up To connect to a host computer by using your modem and a phone line. Contrast this to a dedicated connection.

dial-up direct A connection type that connects your computer directly to the Internet, passing through the host computer. From the computer's point of view, it's the same as a dedicated connection, which means that you can use graphical interfaces to access the Internet. Contrast this with dial-up terminal.

dial-up terminal A connection type that connects your computer to the host computer as a "dumb terminal." In other words, your keyboard and monitor become your means of accessing the host computer, and your own computer's "brain" sits dumbly by and watches. A dial-up terminal is a rather limited way of connecting to the Internet, because it doesn't let you use graphics.

domain name A name given to a host computer on the Internet. The domain name of your host computer will be part of your e-mail address. My address is clarkd@bvsd.k12.co.us. The bvsd is the name of the machine, k12 is my network combined with co (for Colorado) and us (for United States). Collectively, bvsd.k12.co.us forms my domain name.

download To transfer files from one computer to another. When the file is coming to your computer, you're downloading it.

When it's moving from your computer to someone else's, you're uploading it.

Elm A UNIX program used for reading e-mail. Elm is an older program and has limited functionality. Many people prefer Pine, a newer program.

e-mail Stands for electronic mail. A system by which people send and receive messages using their computers over a network (such as the Internet).

emoticon See *smiley*.

Ethernet A common networking scheme used to link computers together so that they can share data.

Eudora An e-mail program for the Mac or Windows that can be used with a direct Internet connection (dedicated or SLIP/PPP). Eudora has a graphical interface that allows the user point-and-click accessibility.

FAQ Stands for Frequently Asked Questions. A document about a given topic in a question-and-answer form.

finger A UNIX program used to find information about other users.

flame An insulting newsgroup posting or piece of e-mail.

follow-up A response in a newsgroup to a posted article.

Freenet A community-based network providing various electronic services, such as Internet access, to local users.

freeware Software that is distributed free of charge by the author, who retains the copyright.

FTP Stands for File Transfer Protocol. A method by which files are transferred over the Internet.

FWIW Stands for "For What It's Worth."

FYI Stands for "For Your Information."

gateway A computer system that transfers data between computers that are running different operating systems.

GEnie An online Information Service that offers all the usual online services, plus some Internet access.

Gopher A piece of UNIX software that allows you to tunnel through the Internet and retrieve information. When entering Gopher, you encounter a menu that helps you navigate the Internet.

gopherspace The arena you are playing in when you fire up your Gopher program.

host A computer connected directly into a network, such as the Internet. When dialing into the Internet, you connect into your host computer and manipulate this machine to surf the Net.

HTML Stands for HyperText Markup Language. It's a simple programming language used in creating World Wide Web home pages.

Hyperlink A selectable piece of text found on a World Wide Web page. When selected and activated, either by clicking with the mouse (for Netscape or other graphical Web browsers) or hightlighting and pressing return (using Lynx), will connect you to another World Wide Web page.

Hypertext A system by which users can jump from site to site around the Internet by means of hyperlinks. Using these links, a user can hop around the Internet and connect to a variety of sites on a topic of interest. The World Wide Web is the Internet's best example of a hypertext-based system.

IMHO Stands for "In My Humble Opinion."

Internet Relay Chat Also known as IRC. A program that lets people join together on the Internet to chat.

IP Stands for Internet Protocol. The standard set of rules by which information zips over the network and lands in the right place (most of the time).

IRC See *Internet Relay Chat.*

ISDN Stands for Integrated Services Digital Network. ISDN is a digital telephone service—the phone lines of the future. Most standard phone lines can't carry digital information (they carry sounds), so digital information from your computer has to pass through a modem on both ends to be translated. An ISDN line eliminates the need for a modem, which in turn speeds up the data transfer.

Kermit A popular frog on *Sesame Street*; also a popular downloading protocol used to move files between computers via modems and phone lines.

LISTSERV It's not an acronym but rather an abbreviation for List Server. LISTSERV is a set of discussion groups that meet through e-mail on the Internet. LISTSERV also refers to the UNIX software that manages the discussions.

login The procedure of making a connection with your host computer. This procedure includes filling in your name and password. Login also refers to the name you use when accessing your host computer.

.login A file that exists invisibly in your home UNIX directory. You can alter this file to make changes to your UNIX account, such as changing the look of your prompt from the boring csh> to something more exciting, such as I exist for you only>.

Lynx A text-based browser for the World Wide Web.

Majordomo UNIX software used to manage discussions via e-mail.

MIME Stands for Multipurpose Internet Mail Extensions. It's a system that uses e-mail to send computer files, such as graphics and video.

mirror site An FTP site that duplicates the holdings of another site. It can be useful if the original site is extremely busy.

modem A device that enables a computer to send and receive data over regular phone lines. A modem converts analog (sound) signals to digital (computer) information, and vice versa. Modems can be built into your computer or can sit as another box on your desk, connected to your computer by a cable.

netiquette   The rules of etiquette governing communication over the Internet. NEVER USING CAPITALS WHEN SENDING E-MAIL UNLESS YOU WANT TO BE PERCEIVED AS SHOUTING is an example of a netiquette rule.

Netscape   A World Wide Web browser that supports graphics, sounds, and video files. It requires a direct connection or direct dial-up (SLIP/PPP) to work.

newsgroup   One of over 20,000 discussion groups found on the Internet focusing on almost any known subject.

newsreader   A program used to read postings or articles from newsgroups.

online mail reader   Just the opposite of offline mail reader. You are connected every moment you are reading and composing. Pine is an online mail reader.

online   When you have a connection to another computer, you are said to be online. Offline is the rest of your life.

OTOH   Stands for "On The Other Hand."

permanent connection   A connection to the Internet using a dedicated, high-speed phone line. Your school's host computer probably has a permanent connection, and if you're using a computer that's directly hooked to it, such as in a computer lab, then you have a permanent connection, too, by association. If you use a modem to dial into the host computer, you don't have a permanent connection.

Pine   A UNIX e-mail program. Stands for "Pine is not Elm." (Elm is an older e-mail program.) Pine is rapidly becoming the UNIX e-mail program of choice because of ease of use.

PPP   Stands for Point-to-Point Protocol. A set of rules for managing a dial-up direct connection.

public domain software   Software that is not owned by anyone. This software may be freely copied, altered, and distributed. Contrast with freeware and shareware.

remote login   The act of connecting with another computer at another location. See *Telnet*.

server   A computer or program that offers a service to another computer or program.

service provider   An organization that offers Internet access to people. These providers charge for their access.

shareware   Software posted in a try-before-you-buy mode. This software is frequently free for the downloading, but if you continue to use it, you are honor-bound (and legally bound) to compensate the author.

shell   UNIX software that processes the commands you give at your UNIX prompt. There are various shell versions available, including the C Shell, Bourne Shell, and Korn Shell. Depending on which shell you use (or which shell was set up for you), the commands you type at your UNIX prompt may vary.

signature   A series of lines at the end of an e-mail or news posting giving information about the author. These lines are usually automatically attached to the posting.

SLIP   Stands for Serial Line Internet Protocol. A set of rules for managing a dial-up direct connection. There are several sets of rules, any one of which will work; SLIP is one, and PPP is another.

smiley   A text version of a smile, such as :) (turn your head to the side). These are used to express emotion in e-mail and UseNet postings. Also called emoticons.

TCP/IP   Stands for Transmission Control Protocol/Internet Protocol. TCP/IP is an agreed-upon system of transferring data over the Internet. To use a dedicated or dial-up direct connection, you must run a TCP/IP program, unless TCP/IP support is built into your operating system.

Telnet A means of logging into other computers on the Internet, as if you were a local user on that system. When *telnetting* to another computer, you frequently will be asked to provide a login name and password.

UNIX A popular computer operating system widely used on the Internet. Many hosts use UNIX as their operating system and require basic knowledge of UNIX commands to get around on them.

upload To transfer a file from your local computer to a remote one. The opposite of download.

URL Stands for Uniform Resource Locator. This is the long-winded addressing system used by the World Wide Web; http://bvsd.k12.co.us/david/family is a short example of an URL.

UUDECODE The changing of UUENCODED files back into their original state.

UUENCODE A method by which DOS and UNIX binary files (such as graphics, programs, and spreadsheets) are transferred into ASCII characters.

Veronica Stands for Very Easy Rodent-Oriented Netwide Index to Computerized Archives. A UNIX utility used to search Gopher menu titles in gopherspace.

virus A potentially damaging program that can be transferred from computer to computer by shared floppy disks or over phone lines. These programs replicate themselves and spread. Virus scanning software and regular backups of your data can prevent you from becoming their victim.

VT100 The standard mode of terminal emulation used by many hosts. Also a product name of a DEC computer.

W3 A shorthand for World Wide Web.

WAIS Stands for Wide Area Information Server. A system that allows users to search a variety of databases on the Internet.

White Pages A partial and growing list of the people who use the Internet.

Whois A UNIX program used for searching for Internet users.

World Wide Web A system of navigating the Internet through preestablished links. The Web operates on a series of home pages set up by schools, governmental and commercial entities, and individuals (such as you and me) around the world. These pages include links to other Internet sites and resources.

WWW See *World Wide Web*.

WYSIWYG Stands for "What You See Is What You Get." The term originally referred to a program that showed you on-screen the exact result you would get when printing your data—for example, a word processing program that showed the various fonts on-screen that would print. Nowadays, the term has expanded to mean any user-friendly, graphical interface.

Xmodem A transfer protocol used to exchange data between computers via a modem.

Ymodem A transfer protocol used to exchange data between computers via a modem.

Zmodem A transfer protocol that includes error checking and crash recovery.

INDEX

Symbols

< > (angle brackets), HTML tags, 127

/ (slash), HTML tags, 127

A

account names, *see* username

accounts

    SLIP/PPP, 10

    UNIX, 4

        dial-up connections, 9-10

address book, e-mail, 31-33

addresses

    domain, mailing lists, 41

    e-mail, 4-5, 19

        suffixes, 20

    Telnet, 5

    Web, 92

Alta Vista Web site, 121

angle brackets (<>), HTML tags, 127

anonymous FTP (File Transfer Protocol), 70

applications, helper, 97

ASCII (American Standard Code for Information Interchange) files, 74

B

binary files, 74

Bookmark command (Window menu), 121

bookmarks, setting, 120-121

browsers, *see* Lynx, Netscape

C

case-sensitivity, UNIX, 146

chat sessions, *see* talk sessions

Choose Newsgroup command (File menu), 102

closing Netscape, 97

commands

    Connect menu, Remote System, 4

    Edit menu

        Mail and News Preferences, 92

        Preferences, 100

    File menu

        Choose Newsgroup, 102

        Exit, 8

        Print, 119

        Save As, 118

        Send Page, 119

    Finger, 151-152

    UNIX, 148, 150, 154

    Who, 152

    Window menu

        Bookmarks, 121

        Discussions, 101

communications programs, 8-10

configuring Netscape, 92-94

Connect menu commands, Remote System, 4

connecting to Internet, 2-6, 8-10

connections

    dedicated, 2-3

    dial-up, 2-3

        to Internet, 8-10

    direct, 2-3

        to Internet, 4-6

    Netscape, requirements, 95

    SLIP/PPP accounts, 2-3

    terminal, 2-3

converting files, 80-82

copying files, UNIX, 149-150

D

decompressing files, 80-82

dedicated connections, 2-3

dial-up connections, 2-3

    Netscape, requirements, 95

    to Internet, 8-10

    UNIX accounts, 9-10

dialog boxes, Save As, 118

direct connections, 2-3

    to Internet, 4-6

directory, home, UNIX, 145-146

Discussions command (Window menu), 101

documents, text, UNIX, 146-149

domain addresses, mailing lists, 41

downloading files

    graphics, 131, 134-135

    with Web, 97-101

E

e-mail

    address book, creating, 31-32

    addresses, 4-5, 19-20

    nicknames, group, assigning, 32-33

    headers, 44

    messages

        deleting, 27-28

        forwarding, 25-26

navigating, 18
printing, 28-29
reading, 23-24
replying to, 25
saving, 26-27
sending, 19-22
signature files, 30
starting, 16-17
Web information, 117-120
see also mailing lists
Edit menu commands
Mail and News
Preferences, 92
Preferences, 100
editors, text
HTML, 139
pico, UNIX documents,
146-148
Ethernet, 2-3
Exit command (File menu), 8
**exiting, UNIX talk sessions,
153-154**

F

File menu commands
Choose Newsgroup, 102
Exit, 8
Print, 119
Save As, 118
Send Page As, 119
files
ASCII (American Standard
Code for Information
Interchange), 74
binary, 74
decompressing/converting,
80-82
downloading
graphics, 131,
134-135
with Web, 97-101
extensions, 74-75, 80, 99
signatures, e-mail
messages, 30
transferring, *see* FTP
UNIX, 149-150
**Finger, users, finding,
151-152**
formatting HTML tags, 131
FrontPage text editor, 139

FTP (File Transfer Protocol)
anonymous, 70
connecting with remote
sites, 70-74
files
decompressing/
converting, 80-82
downloading via
direct
connections,
76-78
downloading via
modem
connections,
78-79
transferring into
UNIX directory,
74-76

G-H

graphics
Auto Load Images option,
turning off, 100
downloading, 131,
134-135,
pages, home, adding to,
133-136

**hardware requirements,
Netscape, 95**
Help menu, Pine, 18
helper applications, 97
**home directory, UNIX,
navigating, 145-146**
home pages
creating, 126-131
graphics, 133-136
hyperlinks, 131-133
tables, 136-138
HotDog text editor, 139
HTML
<> (angle brackets), 127
/ (slash), 127
editors, 139
formatting, 131
home pages
creating, 130
graphics, 133-136
hyperlinks, 131-133
tables, 136-138
tags (HTML), 127

**HTML (HyperText Markup
Language), 126**
**HTML Guides and Tutorials
Web site, 139**
hyperlinks, 90
pages, home, adding to,
131-133
Web, navigating, 95-97
**HyperText Markup
Language,** *see* **HTML**

I-J-K

**Infoseek search engine,
115-117**
Internet
connecting to, 2-6, 8-10
logging off, 8
logging on, 6
**Internet Assistant text
editor, 139**
Internet Explorer, 90
**Internet Explorer shareware
archive Web site, 99-101**

Kermit, 79

L

links, *see* **hyperlinks**
**lists, hyperlinks, home
pages, adding to, 131-133**
LISTSERVs, *see* **mailing lists**
logging off, Internet, 8
logging on, Internet, 6
login name, *see* **username**
Lycos Web site, 121
Lynx, 90
pages, home, graphics,
adding to, 131, 133-136
Web, navigating, 98

M

**Mail and News Preferences
(File menu), 92**
mailing lists
digest option, setting,
45-46
domain addresses, 41
headers, 44
posting to, 43-45